10 Steps to Starting and Running a Successful Business

Avoiding the Pitfalls

Stephen J. Frankel

10 Steps to Starting and Running a Successful Business: Avoiding the Pitfalls
www.theenterprisementor.com
Copyright © 2025 Stephen J. Frankel

Paperback ISBN: 978-1-917640-52-7

All rights reserved. No portion of this book may be reproduced mechanically, electronically, or by any other means, including photocopying, without permission of the publisher or author except in the case of brief quotations embodied in critical articles and reviews. It is illegal to copy this book, post it to a website, or distribute it by any other means without permission from the publisher or author.

Limits of Liability and Disclaimer of Warranty
The author and publisher shall not be liable for your misuse of the enclosed material. This book is strictly for informational and educational purposes only.

Warning – Disclaimer
The purpose of this book is to educate and entertain. The author and/or publisher do not guarantee that anyone following these techniques, suggestions, tips, ideas, or strategies will become successful. The author and/or publisher shall have neither liability nor responsibility to anyone with respect to any loss or damage caused, or alleged to be caused, directly or indirectly by the information contained in this book.

Publisher
https://authorssolution.co.uk/

This book is dedicated to my Uncle Mark, whose kindness, patience, and mentorship shaped my early days in the family business. You showed me the value of hard work, creativity, and vision.

I wish you were here to read it.

To Laura, whose belief in me and generous financial backing gave me the foundation to build a successful business. Your encouragement and support have been invaluable, and I will forever be grateful for the trust you placed in me.

Table of Contents

Acknowledgments vii
Testimonials ix
Foreword xi

Chapter 1
Choosing Your Business 1

Chapter 2
Pros and Cons of a Business Plan 13

Chapter 3
Startup Financing: Creating Income in the Early Days 25

Chapter 4
Finding Customers and Networking 37

Chapter 5
Creating a Supply Chain for Your Business 49

Chapter 6
Using Agencies and Outsourcing to Pay for What You Need 61

Chapter 7
Building Your Team for Growth 73

Chapter 8
Understanding Your Finances to Get Profitable..89

Chapter 9
Do You Really Need to Expand?..101

Chapter 10
Valuing, Selling, and Exiting a Successful Business 113

About the Author..125

Acknowledgments

To my darling wife, Suzanne, whose steadfast love and support have carried me through both the highs and the challenging moments of my business journey. Though my relentless pursuit of dreams may have tested your patience, you never wavered. Thank you for believing in me and for standing by my side through it all then and even now; I couldn't have done it without you!

Secondly, I thank Hirsch Goldblatt, from whom I learned so much about business, and for his inspirational words, "The ability to get things done!" I remember only too well sitting at his house until well after midnight to get a price list completed. That willingness to work hard and not limit myself is what I will always remember about my time with him.

Testimonials

"Stephen has a book I want to encourage you to get. It's your moment, your time to get *10 Steps to Starting and Running a Successful Business: Avoiding the Pitfalls.*"

Les Brown, renowned motivational speaker

"I have known Stephen Frankel for over 30 years. During this time, he has always shown me to be a very caring, thoughtful, supportive friend and business colleague.

"If you are considering starting your own business, I recommend his book: *10 Steps to Starting and Running a Successful Business: Avoiding the Pitfalls.*

"I found it a very enjoyable and valuable read. It explains in very simple baby steps all topics you need to consider before contemplating starting your own business and possibly selling it later down the road. Having been an entrepreneur for over 30 years, he is very open to sharing some of his wisdom and experience to support you. He happily shares some of his winning strategies alongside some of his challenges. This book offers very practical, easy first steps to apply and implement, avoiding many pitfalls that could be very costly.

"Should you be interested in being mentored by him, it would be a beneficial, highly supportive experience to help you achieve your goals more quickly and successfully."

Jenny Lamski, business performance coach

"Stephen Frankel is an experienced entrepreneur and business owner. Bringing his professional experience to the fore, Stephen is now teaching others how to successfully run their own businesses. Not only does he share practical tips, but he also highlights areas where mistakes can be made, helping you to avoid issues that could negatively impact your business. I appreciate his honesty and authenticity."

Gavin Holmes, CEO of Tradeguider Systems International and author of *Trading in the Shadow of Smart Money*

Foreword

Are you ready to start a business but not sure how? Is financing a challenge for getting your business off the ground? Are you struggling with building clientele or having trouble deciding whether or not you should expand? If so, *10 Steps to Starting and Running a Successful Business: Avoiding the Pitfalls* is the guide you have been looking for. With over 30 years of experience in starting and running profitable businesses, Stephen Frankel can mentor you through the early stages of your business and beyond.

Stephen offers practical tips regarding building your team, recruiting and hiring, and marketing your business cost-effectively. He also dives into the pitfalls, helping you avoid mistakes that can lead to financial difficulties for your business. *Avoiding the Pitfalls* covers more than just developing a good business idea. Stephen also shares essential information about financing a startup, plus what you need to know about your financials to make informed decisions and strategically plan for the future.

10 Steps to Starting and Running a Successful Business: Avoiding the Pitfalls is a manual for successfully starting and growing your business. It also provides practical information for valuing your profitable business when you are ready to exit and move on to your next adventure. If you are thinking of starting a business, trying to decide if you want to expand your business, or are ready to exit your business, Stephen has all the lessons and practical experience you need.

Raymond Aaron
New York Times **Bestselling Author**

Chapter 1

Choosing Your Business

Starting a business can be an exciting time. After all, you are choosing to be the boss, creating the foundation of a business that can provide a greater level of security. For many individuals, starting a business is focused on building independence by creating a schedule that allows for personal and family time and greater financial resources, but the process of starting and building a successful business involves more than deciding on a product and selling it.

I have years of experience in starting businesses and running them. Some have failed, some have been profitable, and some have been sold. For me, the goal is to share the mistakes I made, helping you to have a greater level of success as you work to achieve your professional goals.

My mentoring program has been designed to help entrepreneurs through the process of starting and running a business and how to avoid the pitfalls which often occur, so that they can run a profitable and rewarding business.

One of the biggest challenges I see people facing is trying to figure out what type of business they want to run. While it might be easy to start a business based upon a hobby or interest, the truth is that while you might enjoy it, that business could struggle because there is not a real market for the products you produce, or the product is so specialized that the market is not large enough to support the business.

While there is plenty of encouragement to do something you enjoy, you also have to be realistic about the future profitability of the idea. One of the things that I notice is there are trends of items that appear for a time, enjoy a brief level of popularity, and then disappear from the market. The business was not sustainable, so the results were less than stellar. Those businesses quickly end up failing, closing their doors, and potentially leaving you with debt.

So how can you determine the right business to start? There is an element of risk when you start a business, no matter the products or services you offer. Taking certain steps is key to reducing that risk and increasing the likelihood of success.

Let's start by determining a few ways to find the right business and industry to fit your goals.

What Do You Enjoy?

Many individuals find the right business by looking at what they enjoy doing, be it a hobby or pastime, and determining if it can be monetized. The truth is that for the first couple of years, you will be spending a lot of time working on your business. Since you must invest that much time and energy, then it is worth creating a business around something that you already enjoy doing.

Even if you have a good idea, that doesn't mean the idea can be monetized. One individual I mentored gave up a steady job, following his belief that starting an electric car advisory service, which would help people decide what electric car to purchase, would be viable. My first question to him was, "How will you make money off this idea?" While his expertise would benefit potential electric car buyers, he didn't have a clear path to turn his knowledge into income.

After a year of not earning much money and exhausting his savings, he ended up going back to his 9 to 5 job. The truth is that there is a need to plan before you just dive into a good idea. Your business will cannibalize all the money it makes in the early days as you have to reinvest to increase inventory, ramp up marketing, or cover overhead expenses.

Expecting to draw an income from your business can be difficult for you to manage during the first six months to a year. So, when you choose your business, recognize that you need to invest in the business and have funds set aside to pay your bills for a period of time.

I often advise people how they can test their market ideas before they possibly give up their full-time jobs and invest a lot of time and money, and also give them ideas and direction on what business to start and run.

Finding the Gap in the Market

Industries throughout the world have been built around providing a service or product line to consumers, and multiple businesses can be involved in the process. Think about cosmetics. Businesses in that industry might be focused on formulation, packaging, or branding.

For bonuses go to ...

One cosmetic company might work with multiple businesses to create their finished product.

Perhaps you are not the finished product business, but you are providing a piece of the puzzle. Essentially, you find a gap in the market and then fill that gap. That gap might be identified by someone else, but they don't realize the potential or know how to get the business off the ground. Working with them, you can create a viable business, or you can opt to finance the process, buying them out.

McDonald's started out as a small hamburger business, but Ray Kroc saw the potential of the business to grow. He did not have the money to purchase the business, so he used a financial partner, who later became the president of the McDonald's chain. The rest is history. He saw the potential of an idea and invested in growing that potential.

However, finding a gap within an existing industry means you are articulating a problem that you have found, then targeting those businesses that struggle with that problem, and highlighting the solution you offer.

The truth is that many businesses have challenges, but they don't seek out a solution until it becomes a major point of pain for them, negatively impacting their profitability. If you are providing the solution, then you need to highlight how you are making things better, without causing other issues. Software companies have this challenge. They offer a great solution for project management, for instance, but that software might not be compatible with their inventory software or accounting software. The result is that businesses find themselves doing more work to get all their systems to talk with each other. Those types of solutions quickly get abandoned, and it is hard to build a viable business.

If you are filling a gap in the market, then you have to think through the potential challenges that might come up if they opt to implement your solution, and be prepared to address those right away. Your customers need to feel that you can handle any objections.

You are building a business that creates word of mouth within your chosen industry, creating a viable alternative to the current solutions available. Think about Apple as a company for a moment. Apple stepped in and started providing a new way to listen to music. It meant not traveling with CDs or being limited to listening to the same artist over and over.

As the iPod took off, Apple began to create a music platform, then broke into the smartphone industry. Today, they remain a leader, providing a complete platform for entertainment and functionality. They disrupted the entertainment and communications industries and completely altered how we communicate with each other throughout the day.

As you can see, there are ways to break into current industries, but you may also struggle to find a footing, simply because the powerhouse players of that industry do not want to lose market share to a startup. So, you need to be prepared to spend time convincing people to give your product or service a chance. But if it is the right product or service at the right time, you could end up creating a viable opportunity for growing a business.

If you do have a unique product, could you get it patented and then have the potential to sell it to the big players? Some ideas have been sold for many millions, enabling the seller to retire or fund another business.

With that in mind, perhaps you recognize that your solution is not so groundbreaking and disruptive that you can break into a specific industry. Is there another option that can allow for the creation of a business that already exists or has a solid foundation?

Ready for the Franchise?

Many businesses today, particularly in the hospitality and restaurant industries, find it easier to franchise versus opening locations on their own. Those who own one of the franchises are buying your systems, branding, and product line, and your brand grows with their investment.

Think about some of your favorite restaurant chains. Many of them are based upon the franchise model. The corporation produces a set of systems and processes that have been proven to work and then trains the franchise owners on how to operate under that system. It allows them to grow the company without investing in the locations themselves. Plus, they can still have control in terms of the products and services offered. Franchises fuel growth and infuse capital into the main company.

Plus, when you purchase a franchise, you are accessing a business that has proven to be successful already. It will still take an investment of time and energy, but you will benefit from the national advertising campaigns and other efforts made by the corporation to draw in more business. On the other hand, it also means you are restricted to offering only the products of the main corporation, and it limits your ability to expand the business in different ways.

Entrepreneurs can face obstacles during the planning and conceptualizing stages of the business, and it becomes a trial-and-error process to achieve stability and success. Franchises eliminate the guesswork because the main corporation has already done all the work of launching a business from scratch.

Let's talk about a few of the advantages of opting for a franchise:

Proven concept – You know the business is successful, plus you can see the numbers and get insights from those who already are franchisees.

Brand recognition – Consumers trust brands they know and use, particularly when they are traveling or going about their daily routine. A franchise provides consistency because they know what the menu will be and know the products and services will be the same regardless of location.

New industry – Franchising allows you to break into a new industry without going back to school. Your franchisor will teach you what you need to know.

Corporate partnerships and support – Franchisors help franchisees with ongoing education and training. Some even offer lease negotiations, call centers, and administrative support. The franchisors also create strategic alliances and partnerships, which give their franchisees significant advantages. Franchisees might also enjoy approved vendor status and discounts on equipment and inventory.

Built-in network – Franchise owners can feel as if they are part of a larger family when they buy their franchise. Some franchisors even create mastermind groups and special events meant to build cohesion between corporate locations and the franchisees. Plus, being part of this built-in network provides a system that helps to mitigate risk while providing more predictability and support.

But with any business model, there are also potential disadvantages, and that is true of franchises as well. The model requires a significant investment upfront in the form of a franchise fee. The corporation might also have specific requirements that must also be met in terms of building your location. Then you owe royalties based upon the franchise contract. While those fees do cover ongoing support and other resources, some franchisees can find that those royalties impact profitability, and if they do not receive support or other resources, they might find the royalties are a burden.

Along with royalties, you also will have less creative control. If you can't deal with the fact that you are not in control of the menu or can't create a custom advertising campaign, then you might not want to step into the world of franchising.

Your business is also likely to be impacted by factors outside of your control. For instance, a franchisor might allow locations based on territory, population, and the miles between locations. You might find that you are limited in the choice of location or be unable to expand into other areas because territories have been taken by other franchisees. Some franchisees opt to purchase a multiple-location deal so that they can expand their business at a later date when they have the capital to do so.

Bad press aimed at the corporate level can also negatively impact your business. Depending on how the brand is managed overall, you could find that your business takes a significant hit when stories about spoiled food or labor issues pop up. The result is that, even if your location is not dealing with these problems, it will be tarred with the same brush and leave you struggling to stay afloat.

Truthfully, there are tradeoffs when you decide to open a business. Choosing a franchise can give you a leg up, but then you also have to follow the requirements of the corporate office, and your ability to shift directions based on the needs of your business is limited.

As you can see, there are multiple options available to create a viable business. Choosing will depend on what you want to do and how much time and energy you have to develop the business. I know that for some individuals, their business grows as a part-time project until it becomes financially profitable and they can afford to pay a salary to you as the business owner.

There are multiple ways to find a franchise of your choosing; I can of course advise you on this, whether it's magazines or exhibitions or other means.

The question is whether you have the right plan in place to both finance and operate your business. With that in mind, let's talk about a business plan and how it can assist you in the early stages of starting and building your business.

Chapter 2

Pros and Cons of a Business Plan

Building a business involves creating goals and determining a plan to bring those goals into reality. Whether you call it a business plan or a goal, it is a critical part of defining what your business will focus on and serves as a guideline for decision making.

In the past, I have not always created a written business plan with all the various parts as defined below. However, I always had a clear goal of what I wanted to achieve with every business I owned and operated. Whether you call it a business plan or a set of goals, it is important to give yourself something to work to achieve.

As you write down your business plan, recognize that you are doing more than outlining a path to build and grow your business. You are also essentially creating a written vision board for your company. Statistically, written goals are more likely to be achieved versus goals that just stay floating around inside of your head.

The design of your business plan can also give you the ability to set the parameters for your exit. For many people, they are not starting a business that becomes generational. Instead, they have financial goals to achieve before selling or disbanding the business. Having a clear understanding of what you want to achieve can help you to avoid potential distractions that could derail the progress of your company toward achieving your goals.

For bonuses go to ...

With that being said, let's dive into the aspects of a business plan and how they can play a role in defining your next steps.

The Basic Parts of a Business Plan

Business plans document your company's goals and how you intend to achieve them. If you are a startup, your business plan also serves as a way of explaining your business model to potential investors or partners. For established businesses, your business plan becomes a guideline that you refer to regularly, thus ensuring that the choices you are making align with the overall goals of your company.

If you opt for more traditional financing models, having a business plan is an essential part of approaching lenders. They want to see how your business is doing financially right now, but also to get a clear understanding of your strategy for maintaining that financial stability and expanding your market share.

Of course, a business plan gives you a strategy that helps you to focus your energy and achieve viability. Successful companies find it helpful to regularly review the business plan, making adjustments to reflect new goals as old ones are achieved. If you decide to move your business in a new direction entirely, then the business plan needs to be revised to reflect that shift.

Here are some of the benefits business owners have received by taking the time to write up a business plan:

- Thinking through ideas for viability before significant investments occur.

- Highlighting potential obstacles and brainstorming ways to address those obstacles effectively.

- Keeping the executive team united regarding priorities and strategic action items.

- Finding potential gaps in your business model and addressing them early on.

Traditional business plans tend to be longer and heavier on the details because they are designed to be persuasive and reassuring to the stakeholders, including potential investors. Lean startup business plans highlight key elements but are limited in detail. The challenge is that these business plans might leave your investors with questions and require you to provide more detail to answer them effectively.

While no two business plans look exactly alike, there are some basic elements that are found in all business plans. Keep in mind, your business plan should reflect the unique aspects of your company. As a result, some of these areas will have greater levels of detail than others.

Executive Summary

Here is where you introduce your business, its mission statement, and yourself and/or executive team. Your mission statement should explain the purpose of your business. Although you might want to go into great detail, this is where you need to be concise, limiting yourself to a sentence or short paragraph. Your mission statement defines your company's culture, values, ethics, agenda, and fundamental goals, along with how they apply to your stakeholders.

Clearly, this section can pack a punch, showcasing your values and helping investors to see whether their values and goals align with your company. While you might not go into broad detail here, the information you share needs to pack a punch, since it is the first introduction of your business to the wider world.

After your summary, share the goals of your company. Those can be both financial and intangible. For instance, you might want to hit a certain number of followers or raise engagement rates. Although these are not profit-driven goals, they can have a long-term impact on your profitability.

Be realistic with your financial forecast as you can only estimate what your sales and profits are likely to be. It is a fine balance between showing the potential profits to attract an investor and being unrealistic, which will put off an investor or financial institution.

Products and Services

This is where you get into the nuts and bolts of what you do. Are you offering services, products, or a combination of both? Within this section, you can provide details about the products or services, their lifespan, unique benefits to your customers, and the price points.

You also might find it helpful to outline your production and manufacturing processes, such as costs associated with manufacturing, shipping, purchasing of raw materials, research and development, patents, and proprietary technology.

Market Analysis

You may have a fantastic idea for a product or service, but is there a market for it? To be successful at your business, you need a good understanding of the current state of your industry and existing competition. That can help you to determine whether there is a market share out there for you.

Now, you might tweak your products and services a little bit, which then opens up a market share that your competitors were not focused on. However, without an understanding of the current market and demand, you will not be able to determine how your company fits in and if it is worth the time to keep moving forward.

Never ever be put off by opposition or competition! I have been involved in a number of businesses where there are many other companies competing for the same business.

You might win the business for so many reasons; these are just a few:

- "People buy people first." Your prospect might prefer your personality or feel that you are more knowledgeable and trustworthy than another company.

- It could possibly be your location, so that they can get a quick response if need be.

- I have known of many companies selling the same product or services and where they are all making a good living.

I cannot stress this enough, and it is probably the most important section in this book: You must not be put off starting your business, which could be the greatest thing you have ever done for you and your family!

I could spend pages on this subject, but I cover it in much more detail with my mentoring program as some people do need that push for the leap of confidence.

This section is also where you define your ideal customers and how you plan to reach them. Knowing this information assists in determining whether you can easily take market share from your competitors. If you start this process early on, it can make defining your marketing strategy easier.

Marketing Strategy

Here is where you define how you plan to get and keep customers. Your marketing strategy should have advertising and marketing campaigns, distribution channels, and brand messaging. The point is to be clear about how you intend to introduce your company to the world, especially your target audience.

If you are not sure about how you intend to reach out to your target audience, then take the time to do some research so you have a few ideas outlined in your business plan. When you start creating your marketing campaigns, that is when you will get more focused on messaging, costs, and the platforms you will use.

Financial Plans and Projections

For many companies, the financial section of your business plan is essential because this is what investors and lenders look at to determine whether your company is worthy of receiving capital. Established businesses can include their financial statements. New businesses should focus on financial targets and estimates while pointing out where they expect to see the most growth.

If you are making funding requests, this is the section where those requests should be included. The goal is to show that your business has a chance of being financially viable, as well as to demonstrate how your business will achieve stability. You can also highlight the products and services that are likely to be your top earners, as well as areas where you might expand and create future growth.

The best part of business plans is recognizing that they are a reflection of your business, what you hope to achieve, and how you plan to achieve it. Since your business plan is likely to be viewed by potential investors, you want to highlight the potential for viability, expansion, and long-term stability.

You should also be clear about how you plan to execute your vision for the business, how you plan to expand it, and the current financial position of your company. Within this part of the business plan, you are showing that you understand what your business needs to be successful, as well as how you plan to provide for those needs.

On the other hand, if your business is meant to be a short-term endeavor, capitalizing on a specific trend, be clear about that and your expectations. Doing so can help you to target the right type of investors and help you to not overspend throughout the life of your business.

Budgets are also a great way to demonstrate that you understand the financial implications of your company's strategy. Sometimes, new business owners can focus on production and marketing but find themselves struggling to cover overhead because they didn't include that in their costs. To be profitable, the business needs to cover all its expenses and still have funds left over.

Some businesses also include their process strategies, such as software options and the costs associated with opting to use them. The goal is to distill all the information you have about your business, down to what is relevant in a clear and direct manner.

Finally, your business plan needs to outline what your exit strategy is. You might list a few key points, such as the business reaching a specific earning threshold for 5 years in a row or having a specific valuation. Essentially, your business plan should outline its life from beginning to end.

Do Business Plans Fail or Do Businesses Fail?

Business plans are not a recipe for success. Like a beautiful piece of music, it simply has the notes written out. You have to get out the instruments and play the correct notes to achieve a beautiful masterpiece. If you play the wrong note, that is not the fault of the music sheets. The same is true with your business plan. While you can be detailed and write out everything, you still have to act. However, there is a need for flexibility, especially if you are new to a particular industry or market.

In the beginning, your business plan might have unrealistic assumptions and projections. Circumstances outside of your control can impact the success and viability of your business. Markets and economic conditions can change in a way that you didn't foresee. Competitors can bring new products to the market that make yours obsolete.

When these things happen, it does not mean that you should scrap your entire business plan. Instead, you might need to make adjustments to reflect the changing landscape. How are you pivoting your business strategy in terms of products and services being offered? Is your marketing strategy changing?

Larger, older companies that might have begun in the 1980s and 1990s have dealt with these challenges. In the past, they advertised in magazines, newspapers, and on television to reach their audiences. Social media platforms have since blazed a new marketing trail. The result is that companies have transitioned from old marketing platforms to online media.

Years ago, I worked in a family printing business; although successful at the time, we did not move forward with the new technology and eventually ran into trouble.

You must be prepared to upgrade, adapt, and possibly change direction as if you are using a satnav system, to ensure you keep on track and to even try new ideas alongside your current ones.

Recognizing that your target audience is not necessarily using the same media can help you shift your business effectively to increase the ROI for your advertising dollars or pounds. This is just one example of how changes in society can impact your business, requiring you to pivot.

With that in mind, let's talk about how frequently you should revisit your business plan. I would love to say there is a hard and fast rule for regularly revising your business plan, but the truth is that it often depends on your business and industry.

Well-established businesses might just review it once a year, updating financial information and confirming all the other information is still accurate. New businesses, on the other hand, might find it helpful to check out their business plan every quarter to make sure they are still on track with their goals and overall strategy.

Now that you have a plan for how you want to build your company and where you are focusing your marketing efforts, let's turn to what companies find the most challenging, especially in the early days. That's right, we are talking about financing.

Chapter 3

Startup Financing: Creating Income in the Early Days

No matter how good your idea is, no business can function without capital. Whether you invest your funds or seek capital from lending institutions or investors, the goal is to find that initial capital to help your business get off the ground. Realistically, you want that initial investment to help your business reach viability and be able to finance future expansions.

However, the way most traditional financing is provided, startups and small businesses are often ignored because they are seen as too much of a risk. Banks are more eager to lend to businesses that have built a record and have a long financial history. These are the very businesses that are sitting on capital, so they use the financing to preserve capital while still expanding their business.

When you are starting your business, you need to be creative to manage your finances, keep your bills paid, and still make sure the business has what it needs. With that in mind, let's dive into the ways that you can structure the initial financing for long-term success.

Take the Leap to Ownership

Many people who want to own a business get excited about an idea; they dive in and then find themselves struggling to pay their bills.

The business, while it might be growing and generating income, is not generating enough to support you as the owner and pay the costs associated with running the business. The result is that you put your personal finances at risk for the business. If it doesn't succeed, then you have been dealt a double blow.

When I work with new business owners, one of the things I find them struggling with is the financial aspects of managing everything. One of the first recommendations I make is to have a year of their living expenses tucked away before they quit their job and start diving into their business. This gives them a cushion that allows them to focus on getting the business to the point where it is viable, without fearing losses in their personal finances.

That being said, you might be wanting to jump on an opportunity but are not sure that you have enough in your savings to handle the full year of personal expenses. Faced with this challenge, many individuals have opted to work on their business part time while maintaining their current job. The goal is to use their current income to pay personal expenses, so that all the money earned by the business can go back into its expansion and growth.

If you opt to do this, keep track of how the business is doing. Are the orders growing to the point that you can see the income being high enough to support a payroll for staff, including you? If you see the ability to hire someone, then hire yourself.

Of course, if you are excited about your career and do not want to give it up to run your business full time, then you do have the option to hire staff that can handle the daily tasks of the business. This puts you in the mode of an oversight role, thus allowing you to effectively manage the finances of both your business and personal life.

Still, every business reaches a point where expansion cannot happen without an investment of capital, either to purchase new inventory, machinery, or to expand your staff to handle the additional orders. Traditionally, business owners utilize capital raised from the business, but if you have recently started your business, that type of capital can be in short supply.

Throughout this chapter, the focus is on finding ways to tap into capital and financing, both the traditional and non-traditional options. With that in mind, let's start with financial options for startups, especially during those early days when expenses are higher than sales.

Jumpstarting the Financial Foundation

I can honestly say that today's banking options are limited at best for new businesses. Banking institutions want proof that your business is a good return on their investment, but new businesses rarely have that kind of proof. After all, they are likely looking for funding to handle initial production costs, stock purchase, R&D, and marketing. The result is that many of these small businesses end up closing because of a lack of funds, not because the business model is unsound.

When I meet with individuals looking to start a business, I often find them eager to abandon their career and dive into their business full time. The problem is that the business will not be able to support you or give you a salary for months, even up to a year.

That means you need to essentially have the savings in place to cover your living expenses for at least six months while you work on setting up your business and getting those initial sales. However, if your business takes longer to get financially viable, then you could be facing challenges in managing the expenses from the business and your personal life.

One of the ways I have found that individuals succeed in starting a business and still managing their living expenses is by running the business as a part-time endeavor initially. Doing so allows you to keep your full-time job and fund your living expenses, while also determining if the business could eventually be viable. As the business begins to grow, you are now in the position to consider reducing your full-time job to increase the time spent in the business.

Another option to consider is crowdfunding. Today's financial institutions are primarily focused on providing financing options to larger businesses that might not really need the capital, since they have grown in sales and profitability.

Small businesses and startups, on the other hand, who can use this type of financing, find their options rather limited. Crowdfunding platforms can be a source of financing that steps outside of traditional options, thus allowing you to tap into capital for R&D, marketing, manufacturing, and more. These platforms allow you to tap into those individuals who want to invest in ideas and new technologies.

Crowdfunding involves raising money from a large group of people. Those individuals might only contribute a small amount, but once all those amounts are combined, the result is enough funds to move your business forward to the next level.

So, how do these platforms work? Simply put, you can put your business idea out there, and then those who invest can be the first to receive your products, but most of these platforms create a call for donations. The campaign is focused on raising money for a specific goal, thus democratizing access to funding. You no longer need to have connections or bring out financial statements from several quarters to receive the capital necessary to grow your business. Instead, the platform gives you access to a broader audience, allowing you to tap into a large pool of potential backers and market your business at the same time.

Successful campaigns can give you valuable feedback and assist in refining your ideas to get down to the core. The challenge is to stand out from the crowd. Most crowdfunding platforms have many campaigns going for creators, entrepreneurs, and startups. Standing out and gaining visibility can be challenging; however, there are many people out there prepared to give you a chance and give them a return on their money.

If you opt to go this route, then careful planning, dedicated marketing effort, and the ability to deliver on your promises to investors is essential to building a trustworthy and credible reputation.

For bonuses go to ...

Successful Crowdfunding – Team Effort

To be successful in the world of crowdfunding, you need to be focused. The best campaigns spent time on each of these areas, finding the right fit for their business and the right audience.

Although I have listed quite a few things to consider, my personal advice is to use an agency that works with the crowdfunding platforms. They will help you select the right crowdfunding campaign and give you total guidance in preparing your campaign and much more!

Initial consultation usually costs nothing but can be an enormous boost to you getting started, and their costs are small compared to the significant funds that can be raised.

This is also a big subject and could be crucial in starting a business, which I cover in depth when mentoring.

Selecting a Platform

Not all crowdfunding platforms are alike. They have different pricing and fee structures, which can play a role in determining which one is the right option for your business.

Platforms also have different options, which can make them easier to use for potential donors. If the platform is too complicated, then donors will quit in the middle of the process and leave you unable to achieve your goals, because your financing campaign is not successful.

Another point to consider when choosing a platform is whether they offer customization options that allow you to match your campaign with other branding efforts for your organization. Doing so will assist you to create an identity for your business, while also communicating your call to action, your mission statement, and your values.

As you explore a potential platform, you need to check out their tutorials, resource guides, and FAQs. Having these resources available can make it easier for you to navigate the platform, as well as being more user-friendly for your potential donors.

Finally, before you choose a platform, try out their customer support. You want to ensure they are helpful and responsive to your questions, because that means they will provide that level of service for your potential donors.

Fulfilling the Platform's Requirements

Once you choose a platform to work with, then you need to review their requirements to ensure you qualify to use the platform. While requirements can vary from platform to platform, there are a few that consistently come up, such as:

- Being 18 or older.

- Being a permanent resident of one of the platform's eligible countries.

- Having an address, bank account, and government-issued identification in the country where the project is being created.

When the platform accepts you, then you will need to pitch your project to their team, thus ensuring their platform is a good fit for what you hope to achieve. To prepare for the pitch, be proactive in identifying your campaign narrative and laying out your marketing plan. This is your opportunity to sell your business and garner support.

If your campaign is accepted and moves forward, then you can eventually take the funds raised and put them to use. However, some platforms will only release the funds if you meet your campaign goal, while others allow you to withdraw all the funds raised, even if you didn't reach your goal. Knowing what the platform allows can play a role in determining if they are the right platform for you.

Types of Crowdfunding

There are several different types of crowdfunding available. When someone contributes to your business in exchange for something, this is rewards-based crowdfunding. Startups can use this option to offer free swag or discounted services to potential investors. Equity-based crowdfunding, on the other hand, means you essentially give away a percentage of your business for an investment. Keep in mind that when you opt to use equity-based crowdfunding, you are taking on partners. How you handle that can depend on the platform, since you are essentially selling shares.

Donation-based crowdfunding is the simplest form of this process, since your donors are giving with no expectation of receiving something for their donation.

Clearly, crowdfunding can make it easier for your startup to amass capital and market your business to a large audience. Investors want a company they invested in to do well so that it makes them an unpaid sales force, who talk about your company, products, services, and initiatives. Organic conversations like these can lead to greater brand awareness and encourage future customers to take the leap and buy your products or services.

Social media and your crowdfunding platform can be used together to spread the word about the opportunity to fund your emerging business, while highlighting the perks and incentives for doing so. The combination of social media with crowdfunding means that once you have someone interested in your business, you can use the crowdfunding platform to convert them into a donor or investor.

Clearly, as a new startup, you are looking for ways to build your financial foundation. Crowdfunding and savings are two ways to do so. As your business grows and becomes established, then you have more opportunities to tap into capital from traditional funding sources.

But having the funds to get your business off the ground only goes so far. You need to build a customer base that allows you to generate sales and increase the overall profitability of your business. How to build sales and market your business effectively is the focus of our next chapter.

Although I have listed quite a few things to consider, my personal advice is to use an agency that works with the crowdfunding platforms. They will help you select the right crowdfunding campaign and give you total guidance in preparing your campaign and much more!

Initial consultation usually costs nothing but can be an enormous boost to you getting started, and their costs are small compared to the significant funds that can be raised.

This is also a big subject and could be crucial in starting a business, which I cover in depth when mentoring.

I have repeated these paragraphs as it is important NOT to be put off by the work needed, as this can be done by the agency and will normally cost you nothing to investigate this.

Chapter 4

Finding Customers and Networking

You have an amazing product and quality services to offer, but customers are not going to know it if you don't have a solid marketing strategy. The problem with marketing today is that it has evolved to another level. Now, instead of buying some ad time and hoping perspective customers see it, there are tools available to target your customer base and connect with them in a measurable way.

AI can revolutionize marketing by personalizing customer interactions, predicting market trends, and optimizing ad placements. It enables businesses to create targeted campaigns, track customer behavior, and refine strategies in real time, enhancing customer engagement and driving higher conversion rates.

Let's dive into how to do so effectively and build a network that can assist you in growing your business.

What Is Your Target?

New businesses in today's economy can have a vast audience. Some focus on a local customer base since their products or services are more likely to appeal to a specific region. Think about your local bakery. Their cookies, cakes, and other treats are delicious but not

For bonuses go to ...

likely something to be sold around the world. Instead, they would focus on finding ways to interact with their local community and building their brand to encourage people to shop with them for daily bread and treats for special occasions.

Breakfast meetings or breakfast clubs can be a great way to meet other business owners while also promoting your business. These clubs discuss challenges unique to the local community, thus giving you a chance to see what the community needs and how your business can meet those needs.

Take the opportunity to look for local networking events targeting business owners within the area, such as connecting with your local Chamber of Commerce or other organizations targeting small and local businesses. You might find businesses where you can partner, tapping into their customer base and offering them the chance to tap into yours. Both businesses have a chance to grow

Another option for connecting with your local customer base is buying ad space within the local area. With the advent of social media, you can also purchase targeted ads for individuals in your area, which allows you to measure engagement. These ad platforms allow your business to be where the potential customers are, engaging with them more than you can with a traditional advertising medium, such as billboards or newspapers.

That being said, do not be quick to dismiss those options. Depending on your target audience, billboards and newspapers are still viable options to reach customers. The truth is that advertising and marketing for new customers can be based upon a generational strategy.

My parents were newspaper readers. Perhaps you can think about the different generations still relying on newspapers and television for their information. Then you look at younger generations that have grown up on the internet. They constantly rely on their phones and tablets for information from social media or various websites.

Leaflet drops to local businesses can help you reach customers while also building connections within the community. This can be a cost-effective method of reaching out within your geographic area. The best part is that you can do the leaflet dropping yourself or have a few friends walk to different businesses and give them some leaflets to hang up or hand out. The best part is that you can buy them on the internet cheaply, making this an appealing option for new businesses or startups.

If your target audience is the local businesses, you can use the leaflet drop method to let them know about your services, or you could opt to call on them directly and offer your services. These cold calls might not get you a high rate of return, but they can get your name out there, which could turn into customers who opt to purchase your services later.

Another option for getting your business out there is local exhibitions. What is interesting is that these exhibitions are not just a place for you to sell your services; you can also connect with other businesses that offer products or services you need for your business. Exhibitions work two ways. You can visit to get ideas or make contacts. Please do not assume it is a place to sell yourself as you meet people at exhibitions, since those businesses paid to be there in order to sell their services. You have to use your judgment, as some small companies might be interested in your services or products, and they might be willing to talk to you as you move through an exhibition hall.

One method I have used is to take a felt tip pen and mark up the exhibition list of vendors as I move through the hall. I note who I would like to make contact with and then reach out after the event is over. By walking the exhibition, I get a clearer idea of their business and how I can best market it to them.

Knowing the audience that you want to reach is key to building a successful marketing campaign geared toward your local region. Knowing where your target audience is can help you determine the best places to reach them.

I always think of a prospect having a "so what" bubble, as they are thinking, "Why should I be interested in what I am being told or offered?"

On the other hand, global businesses are targeting a significantly larger audience. So, your marketing approach will be different. This might involve tapping into social media, networking, and industry conferences. The type of media you use for your marketing is focused on increasing your reach so that you can target a larger audience. However, having a global reach can also be more expensive. For instance, you can utilize Google Adwords, but that can be pricy, especially for new businesses.

I suggest you find a local, small marketing company to assist you with your advertising and marketing. They can help you with various paid advertising options available online, as well as SEO (search engine optimization), which can help you to get those free ads because your website or social media posts match the keywords being searched by individuals or businesses.

When you focus on marketing for a global audience, you must identify the customers who would most appreciate your products or services and figure out where they are most likely to hang out. Then you need to be present, either with information that answers their questions, or events or discussions meant to get their point of view. Engaging with your target audience helps them see your company as a solution to their issue, even if they didn't realize they had an issue or problem to start with.

Basically, you are competing against other companies to get the prime position on the search results page. Those at the top are paid ads, but you can organically be on that first page of results with the right effort in terms of your content strategy. SEO takes time to move up the ranks, so it will depend on how quickly you want to get going, whether you opt to spend the money on paid ads or not.

Paying for lists can be another effective way to contact companies or businesses you want to target. You can mail them a flier or other information and then follow up with a call from the person in charge of selling at your company. The goal is to break the ice, so when your sales team connects with this company, they already know who you are and have at least a vague idea of what it is that you do.

Telemarketing is another option for getting leads and freeing up your time to spend on quality opportunities. Companies in India and other countries can be hired relatively inexpensively to handle cold calling, thus generating leads for your salespeople to follow up with businesses that are already interested in learning more about what you offer. Telemarketing allows you to focus on other aspects of your business while leads or sales are being generated, thus maximizing your company's efficiency.

Regarding a global reach, exhibitions can serve as a way to introduce yourself to various industries. But it is not just about exhibiting your company. It would help if you also visited and listened to the other sales pitches, learning about what is being offered so you understand what they need and if your products or services are a good fit. You can pick up a lot of good customers through exhibitions if you are willing to put in the work.

Cold calling is an option, but if you are trying to do it on a national scale, it can be more difficult—you will be traveling long distances with no guarantee that you will be able to meet with the business you are targeting or come away with any sales. The challenge with cold calling is that you do not have a guaranteed opportunity to meet with the decision makers of your target customers.

One of the biggest issues with cold calling is that you cannot guarantee that you will connect with the company. Networking can be a way to make your cold calling more effective, because you can receive an introduction from someone who is already familiar with you and your offerings.

The best option for global or national sales is to focus on the methods that allow you to get the most return on investment (ROI) out of every dollar or pound spent on marketing. Your goal is to concentrate your time and attention on customers that are most likely to buy and thus generate sales. You also want to encourage them to talk about your business by offering high-quality customer service.

Many startups often overlook the power of customers talking about their experiences with your business. The more positive experiences you can generate for your target customers, the more likely they will refer other potential customers your way. Reviews and referrals are the lifeblood of any business, especially one looking to break into niche markets or looking to service businesses (B2B).

Long-standing companies understand that it costs more to get a customer initially than it does to keep a customer. Spending money on quality customer service assists you in this process. Plus, happy customers are the ones who bring other customers to your business. For startups or small businesses looking to expand their reach, this can be an effective way to build your clientele without actively spending your marketing budget.

The reality is that no one goes looking for a solution unless the problem creates a big enough pain point that they want to solve it. So, your goal is to help your target audience see that your products or services offer the solution they need. How can you do that effectively while also targeting the largest possible audience?

Write a Book on Your Specialty

Part of what makes a business stand out is the experience and knowledge of its executive team, including the sales staff and leadership. You want to establish your authority within your industry to help customers trust that your business can provide the solutions they need.

For bonuses go to ...

Writing a book can be a great way to highlight your experience and specialization. Being a published author transfers a greater level of authority, thus allowing you to connect with various individuals and companies who become familiar with you through your writing.

Many publishing opportunities abound for you to get yourself published, and you can utilize many tools to assist you, from a professional writer or editor to a self-publishing option, such as Amazon. Once you get published, make sure you talk about it on your social media and your company's website. The goal is to use the book to make connections and highlight your ability to provide services or products that create solutions.

Of course, initially, your book might be money spent without a high ROI. However, your book can also include information about what you do and what your startup is about, and provide a small amount of free advice. All of these options can tap into your target audience's curiosity, making them want to connect with your team to find out more.

Exhibitions also like to have round tables or keynote speakers who share trends in the industry or teach specific skills. After publishing a book, consider exploring speaking engagements at the exhibitions you will attend as an exhibitor or visitor. Doing so provides opportunities for you to get to know potential customers and highlight your offerings less traditionally, so that they don't necessarily feel like they are getting a sales pitch.

Educate By Creating Quality Content

When discussing the sales funnel, one of the most critical aspects is educating your customers about who you are and what you offer. Today, businesses needing assistance with a particular issue start by researching online. They may even first connect with a company through its website as they look for potential solutions to a problem, where the symptoms are apparent but the root cause is not clearly defined.

The question here is whether your website is up to date and whether it is providing what they need in order to do their research and take the next step, which is connecting with your sales team. Instead of considering your website an afterthought, you must make it a front-and-center part of your marketing plan. That means putting up information with keywords your target audience will likely search for and answering questions they are likely to ask.

Highlight your experience and expertise, not necessarily all of your products and services. Your website might be the first time a potential customer interacts with your company, so make sure it is an excellent experience for them.

Building your network and connecting with your customer base is key to building your business, but once you start getting sales, your supply chain comes under scrutiny. Can you meet deadlines and deliver on your sales team's promises? Let's dive into how to create and manage your supply chain effectively.

For bonuses go to www.theenterprisementor.com

Create a Website

A website is essential for your new business as it establishes online presence, increases credibility, and provides a platform for customers to learn about your products or services. It enables 24/7 accessibility, enhances marketing efforts, and facilitates customer engagement, ultimately driving growth and success in the digital age.

Chapter 5

Creating a Supply Chain for Your Business

Starting a business involves deciding what you want to offer your customers and determining what makes your products or services stand out from the competition. However, once you start generating sales, your company's reputation will rely on whether you can deliver the quality product you advertised.

Creating a supply chain involves finding the right manufacturers, warehousing, and fulfilment options to meet your customers' needs and ensure that your products are delivered on time with the highest quality. So, how can you start this process and ensure that your supply chain costs do not price you out of the market?

Understanding the Costs

China and India are manufacturing powerhouses, where production can be completed cost-effectively, making these regions valuable resources for small businesses and startups. However, you must look at how much shipping back to your country will cost, including taxes, import and export costs, and storage and port fees.

Here is why this can be so important to understand: You are pricing your products based on the entire cost of manufacturing and shipping. Those costs to receive the product from another country should be incorporated into your overall cost per unit. Once you have the cost per unit, you can determine if making it closer to home would be cheaper.

How can you find a manufacturer in China or elsewhere? Specific companies offer lists of manufacturers with information about the products they can produce and the materials they can work with.

For instance, you can access lists that allow you to source goods from China and find the manufacturer you need for your products. A word of warning: Agents can buy manufactured goods, then put themselves on the list to sell to businesses, creating a middleman. While this might work for certain products, you might find it unhelpful if you want to change your product line or address quality issues.

If you buy from a trading company, they could change the source where the product is made, and you have no control over this. When you buy directly from the manufacturer, you are guaranteed to get a quality product that is the same every time. So, you need to do a bit of research and contact companies directly if you want to have a greater level of control during the manufacturing process.

The biggest challenge of buying directly from the manufacturer is that they might want you to purchase large quantities, which might not be something that you can handle in terms of storing that much inventory or being able to sell it quickly enough to minimize your holding costs.

We have worked with a wholesaler for some products. They manufacture large quantities and then put them into stock, allowing smaller companies to purchase them without overstocking their business. To get the best options out of manufacturing, you need to understand your sales numbers so that you can order the right amount for your business and not have a significant amount of capital tied up in inventory. Working with a wholesaler can give you an advantage in pricing without making you buy in bulk.

Working with an agent can provide better communication and support for your purchasing. We also have a purchasing manager in China who can source, inspect, and control production and exports.

Creating your supply chain also involves more than finding the right manufacturer. You also need to understand importing and exporting, as the costs of doing business internationally can impact the profitability of your business.

Importing and Exporting – What You Need to Know

With the rising manufacturing costs in the UK and other developed nations, many businesses have turned to developing nations to manufacture their products since the labor and material costs are significantly lower. If you opt to do this, then it is essential to understand the laws and regulations surrounding importing and exporting internationally.

Essentially, you would pay for the goods to leave one country and pay again for those goods to enter another country. Therefore, it is critical that you understand and follow the import/export laws for each country that you will be dealing with. International shipping today also involves ships and planes entering and leaving multiple countries before they reach their final destination.

Let's plan an imaginary vacation for a moment. Likely, if you are leaving the UK to go to Australia, you will have at least one stop or layover. If you leave a specific area of the airport at your stop, then you have to go through customs and security to enter the gate and board your plane.

You will likely have a similar layover when you purchase manufactured goods from one country and bring them to another. Depending on the process, your goods may also require paperwork from you to continue their journey.

There are several types of duties and tariffs that you will encounter as your goods move from the manufacturing country to your country and business. Custom duties are taxes on imported goods when crossing a country's border. These duties vary based on product characteristics, such as material composition, origin, and assembly location.

The Harmonized Tariff System (HTS) provides duty rates for virtually every item. Experts spend years learning how to classify items correctly to determine their duty rates. Remember that the actual duty rate is determined by each country's government and not the importer.

Tariffs are government-imposed direct taxes on specific classes of imports or exports. They apply to products coming in from other countries. The HTS codes under which imported items are classified are referred to as tariffs. Tax rates, such as Value-Added Tax or Goods and Services Tax, are fixed and calculated based on the total value of the imported products. Unlike duties and tariffs, tax rates are not specific to individual products or countries. Remember, each country has its own fee obligations, rules, and forms related to customs duties and tariffs.

Naturally, you might feel overwhelmed by the prospect of importing products from a manufacturer in another country. Still, it is possible to navigate the world of imports and exports without bankrupting your business. It involves tapping into experts who understand this world.

Many businesses today recognize that multiple regulations and laws can affect the movement of their goods before they reach the final destination. With that in mind, they opt to work with an international freight forwarder and customs broker. These companies can handle getting your goods shipped promptly, and ensure that all the correct paperwork has been filed and the appropriate payments have been made.

Some of the paperwork that is required includes a pro forma invoice that contains details like quantity, price, weight, and specifications; a commercial invoice that clearly states the goods being sold and the amount the customer must pay to determine duties and assess the true value of the goods; a packing list with detailed information about the seller, buyer, shipment details, itemized quantities, package type, net/gross weight, dimensions, and package marks; and a certificate of origin that is a signed statement about the origin of the export item.

For bonuses go to ...

A packing list is not a substitute for a commercial invoice. Both must be present and align with each other to avoid any potential delays. A certificate of origin is also not required by all countries and organizations, and only organizations like the local chamber of commerce can validate it. Specific paperwork requirements may vary from country to country, so having a customs broker assist you can minimize delays with receiving your shipment, because they will manage the paperwork and file the appropriate information with the port authorities.

You can find a reliable customs broker and freight forwarder by searching online directories and platforms that provide a list of top global ocean forwarders, along with their logistics revenue, container volumes, and air cargo metrics. Look for forwarders with a strong track record, industry expertise, and positive customer reviews.

Consider the industries and sectors the forwarder specializes in. Some may focus on specific niches or have expertise in handling certain types of shipments. Evaluate whether their expertise aligns with your business needs. Check where the forwarder is headquartered and how many locations and countries they operate in. Ensure they serve the countries you trade with or have your goods manufactured in. A local presence can be beneficial for efficient operations.

Not every freight forwarder offers customs brokerage, so be sure you understand the solutions they provide beyond basic shipping services. Do they offer customs brokerage, cargo insurance, and other value-added solutions?

Seek reviews and feedback from other customers that have used their services. Are they usually on time? How is their customer support? Do they have certifications and industry recognition? All of this can help you to determine if they will provide the services you need and can get your goods into the country without significant delays.

Don't be tempted to use a shipping agent in the country of origin of your goods that offer low shipping costs. Often, they have UK agents who pass commission back to the agent, and you cannot get your goods until you pay their high charges.

Always get a delivered price to your door, including charges and perhaps excluding duty and tax. You can get quotes from the country you're sending to well in advance of purchasing any goods.

With the ongoing changes to weather patterns and continued political shifts worldwide, you need to create a supply chain involving contingency plans in case your shipments are delayed due to events outside the manufacturer and shipper's control.

Creating a Contingency Plan

I encourage business owners who import and export goods to complete supply chain risk management (SCRM). This process helps to identify, assess, and mitigate risks within your company's supply chain. SCRM aims to minimize the impact of potential vulnerabilities on a company's operations, reputation, and financial performance, thus ensuring continuity and resilience by addressing those risks proactively.

Globalization has made supply chains intricate and interconnected. As COVID-19 showed the world, when manufacturing in one country is shut down or drastically reduced, it can have a ripple effect across the globe. Companies rely on suppliers, manufacturers, distributors, and logistics professionals worldwide to get goods and finished products to their final destination on time and in quality condition.

However, the complexity of today's supply chains has also increased the points of potential disruption. Several types of risks can impact your supply chain, especially if you are receiving finished products from a local supplier and not importing anything.

Global events – Natural disasters, geopolitical instability, trade disputes, and economic fluctuations

Supplier risk – Weaknesses in supplier financial stability, capacity constraints, or reliability

Cybersecurity threats – Vulnerability to cyberattacks, data breaches, and system disruptions

When you create a SCRM for your business, you can avoid or minimize disruptions to your supply chain by identifying alternatives for suppliers, manufacturers, and distributors. With a contingency plan available, you can be flexible and adapt to the changing circumstances. This can also make you aware of different manufacturers, suppliers, and distributors, which can give you the ability to reduce costs, improve quality, and enhance your customers' satisfaction with your business. You also comply with regulations, protect your brand's reputation, and foster sustainability for your business.

Customers might read about the disaster or political upheaval in their newsfeed, but they do not want it to impact their ability to fulfill their orders. Contingency plans for your supply chain can be the insurance that helps you keep your customers happy and maintain your company's sales income.

As you build your contingency plan, one of the first things to consider is what products are coming from overseas and what is made locally. For example, you might have specific car parts made overseas, but the car is assembled within the UK. When you build your contingency plan for your supply chain, identify potential suppliers who can provide replacements should your products be delayed in the shipping process, thus allowing you to maintain your schedule and meet your customers' expectations.

Develop a comprehensive emergency business continuity plan and consider each scenario as it impacts your supply chain, including disrupted transportation routes, damaged facilities, and communication breakdowns. Identify critical personnel, designate roles, and establish communication channels. Assess essential supply lines and dependencies within your supply chain.

Regularly back up important data, including inventory records, supplier information, and logistics details. Ensure data redundancy and accessibility from alternative locations. Review existing insurance policies to understand the coverage, deductibles, and limits if you were to make a claim for lost or damaged goods.

Maintain a list of stakeholders, such as employees, banks, lawyers, accountants, and suppliers. Ensure these stakeholders are informed of the information they need regarding any delays or disasters that impact on your shipments. Remember, preparation is vital. By proactively addressing these aspects, you can enhance your supply chain resilience and minimize the impact of disasters or political upheaval on your business.

As your business develops and sales increase, your supply chain might not be the only thing you need to consider. In fact, your company might be poised to expand, but how can you do that successfully if you don't have a team to assist? Let's dive into what you need to know as you hire staff to grow your business.

Chapter 6

Using Agencies and Outsourcing to Pay for What You Need

When starting a new business, part of the journey is understanding what you should keep in-house and what could be outsourced to manage your financial resources better. Today, agencies and outsourcing are a way of life for many different businesses, providing accounting, marketing calls, packing and shipping, and marketing. Your business can truly benefit from these types of services, particularly if you have one fixed monthly cost and can reduce the costs associated with hiring additional staff.

Businesses spend a great deal of capital on inventory and staff. Hiring staff is about more than just their salaries. You must provide them with a workplace, equipment, benefits, and resources. When you opt to have a larger staff, your business is incurring those costs, which might not match up with the current income level.

Outsourcing and agencies can provide you the best way to mitigate these costs initially, allowing you to grow your sales before you start adding staff and the financial implications of building your team. Let's dive into a couple of areas where agencies and outsourcing can benefit your business and help it to grow.

For bonuses go to ...

Packing and Shipping Orders

If you are starting your business while maintaining your full-time position, the idea of spending all your free time packing orders, getting them shipped, and dealing with returns might sound daunting. Outsourcing can provide you another option that allows you to maintain your full-time job, grow your business, and yet not be forced to spend hours every day fulfilling orders and handling their shipment and delivery.

Amazon has developed this business, but plenty of other warehousing options are available to meet your business's needs. Simply put, they house your inventory, and when an order comes in, their team packs and ships it for you. Their software lets you track packages and share that information with your customers. Plus, you have the ability to see what is currently available in your inventory and determine, based upon your sales, when you need to restock specific items.

Now imagine if you had to pay for a warehouse, staff to pack orders, shipping costs, and handling the returns; it would be a significant cost to your business. Today's warehousing and fulfilment companies offer you an option to outsource all those tasks without compromising the customer's experience.

Additionally, warehousing and fulfilment centers can scale up with the demand, which can be valuable during peak seasons and assist you in expanding to additional markets. You can handle sales right from home or on the road, knowing that the order will be fulfilled quickly, and the customer will receive exactly what they bought.

In addition to cost savings and scalability, you also can minimize the risk of processing errors, such as shipping the wrong product or misplacing inventory. Often, in centrally located distribution centers, these services use advanced technology and streamlined processes to ensure accurate and timely order fulfilment, thus increasing customer satisfaction, ultimately leading to more sales.

You specialize in an industry, offering a particular product to your customers. Third-party logistics provides specialization in warehousing and fulfilment. They have the expertise to optimize processes, manage inventory, and handle logistics efficiently. You can focus on your core competencies while leaving warehousing tasks to experts, thus boosting your team's overall productivity.

Outsourcing eliminates the need to invest in warehouse infrastructure, equipment, and technology. These services allow your business to adapt to changing distribution needs without major disruptions. Ultimately, taking on this type of outsourcing allows you to focus on growth and strategy while also freeing up internal resources. Using warehousing and fulfilment options, you can also pass on cost benefits to your customers, creating more competitive pricing that can draw in additional business.

These are just a few of the benefits of outsourcing your packing and fulfilment. However, benefits for your business can also be found when you use agencies to care for specific services.

For bonuses go to ...

Agencies Build Your Skill Set

The truth is that many startups and small businesses lack the resources to compete for the top talent in sales, accounting, and human resources. Instead of trying to compete with larger companies for these skill sets, agencies can give you access to them without your business having to pay the costs associated with current market rates for highly skilled and knowledgeable staff.

Agencies today can provide you with accounting services to help you navigate bookkeeping, taxes, and other financial services. Some agencies can even offer you access to a CFO, allowing you to benefit from their strategic thinking without the high-dollar price tag.

You might also be surprised to learn that agencies handle human resources, including recruiting, hiring, and onboarding, as well as managing your benefits packages for the team members you choose to hire. Human resources agencies have streamlined their hiring process, so instead of it taking weeks or months for you to find the best professional for your company, they can have the position filled in weeks or even days if it is a temporary hire.

Additionally, these agencies have a greater candidate pool to pull from, which gives you more options to find the right fit and level of expertise for your company. As you grow your company, these agencies can scale up with you, allowing for flexibility during busy seasons and for you to reduce costs when your demand slows down.

Plus, these agencies manage the continuing education of their workforce, so you do not have to incur the costs of sending your employees to workshops, seminars, and other continuing education opportunities. The result is that your business has access to top talent without a significant outlay of capital.

Another benefit for your business is that outsourcing certain roles means your business is not incurring costs of a full-time employee when there is not enough work to justify that role. In bookkeeping, for example, you might have enough work for a few hours each week, but hardly enough to hire someone in-house. Instead of trying to make time for handling the bookkeeping yourself, you can outsource it and have professional work done in an affordable manner.

If you want someone to answer the phone, handling basic questions for both leads and customer service, answering services could be the right fit. These services can answer in your name when individuals call your business number, taking messages and answering questions based upon a script that you have given them. This allows for better overall customer service and can allow you to focus on the more complex issues related to your customers, such as product questions or troubleshooting. After getting off the phone, they can send you a WhatsApp or email with the contact details. You can opt to have them answering all your calls or only between certain hours. This way, you never miss a call, and it is inexpensive. There are also answering services that can kick in after your business hours. The costs of these services are based upon different plans, so you would get so many calls for free and then have a base rate per call, which can make it a cost-effective option to make sure that your phones are always answered.

Another way to use these services is to set up proxy addresses within a country or area where you want to expand. A little bit of targeted advertising and your answering service can help you to determine if there is interest. You can use this information to decide if you want to invest capital in an expansion or if there is insufficient interest to warrant that level of investment. Using answering services in this way is a minimal cost but can bring you much critical information to assist you in strategizing your business.

In my years in business, I have seen how agencies and outsourcing can play a crucial role in a startup or small business. They offer services that relieve the owner of pressure, allowing them to focus on scaling the business up and growing sales. Let's explore a few other areas where you might use outsourcing and agencies in multiple aspects of your business, from marketing to cold calling for potential leads.

Outsourcing for Marketing and Advertising

Having your own in-house marketing team is usually difficult because having that level of talent within your company can cost a significant amount of capital. Outsourcing your marketing means you can find companies that specialize in different areas of marketing, such as SEO, digital marketing, and building a high-quality website.

Having a point person on your team for marketing can allow for cohesion without negatively impacting on your budget. The result is that your company is still in charge, but you are outsourcing the skills and creativity of a larger team.

One company of mine took this approach to maximize its marketing budget. They had their website done very cheaply by a company in

India, then the SEO was done by another company, and another company handled the pay-by-click. Each specialized in different areas, but they all came together to create a solid marketing strategy.

Outsourcing and agencies give you access to a variety of talent, allowing you to make your vision come true even during a startup's lean years or with a smaller budget associated with a small business. As your business grows and the objectives change, do not feel as if you can't move away from one company and move to another.

This type of outsourcing allows your company to adapt to changes in the market and the flexibility to change direction in your marketing fairly quickly. Another option is using one company to start the process before dividing the work among several marketing companies. When starting a business, outsourcing and agencies are a way to maximize your capital and get your name out there to increase sales and drive your income up.

Another marketing option is a PR company, which can help you get your name out there and focus on building your brand's reputation within the industry. They can also get you write-ups in trade magazines, which can be extremely helpful if your products or services are unique to your industry.

For a service-oriented business, like a financial advisor, a PR company can assist in getting a write-up in a local newspaper or magazine, highlighting the benefits of its service to individuals looking to invest. The goal of the PR company is to ensure the write-up focuses on the best aspects of the business, showcasing your expertise by highlighting current legislation or other changes within the industry, and could incorporate a call to action.

For bonuses go to ...

Outsourcing the Cold Calls and Initial Contacts

To grow a business, you must increase initial sales and find ways to bring back repeat customers. Telephone marketing can help get your name out there and increase leads, but the challenge for you as a new business owner is that you do not have hours each week to spend on the phone, essentially cold calling potential customers.

Outsourcing your telemarketing can be a great way to maximize the benefits of time and energy while still positively impacting your sales numbers. The agency's employees spend time on the phone, trying to connect with customers, while you focus on other business areas that benefit from your attention.

Companies out of India offer these services at competitive rates, but it is important to research to find the right agency to work with your company and make sure they can meet the numbers you need to succeed. If possible, set up a trial period so you can see if they are meeting expectations. Do not be afraid to move to another company if you are not seeing results or if the agency is not responsive to your needs.

After all, if you spend money on a telemarketing agency, you want to know that it is the best investment of your business capital and will have the highest ROI possible. You can have your telemarketing agency work on several different tasks for your company. They might gather information about potential customers, generate leads, or basically target anything that you would want.

Another option as part of your marketing efforts would be to buy mailing lists, setting out the specific metrics you want the list to have.

This allows you to purchase lists that are more likely to have your target audience in the mix. Before you purchase a list, check to see what the agency's reputation is for up-to-date information. If a list is outdated, it is unlikely to generate the leads you need to make sales.

There are several types of lists that might be available, including ones that allow you to create an email with critical information about your business and links to your website, which you can then send out in an email blast. You might also opt to send marketing materials via post, but the ability to measure their effectiveness might be limited.

A company like Mailchimp or Constant Contact can take a list you bought and, once exported into Excel, can turn it into a marketing opportunity. When you use companies such as the above, you upload the list you bought and then use their software to create a mailer, using one of their templates if required. Once the mailer is created and approved, the company gets it emailed from your list.

The beauty of using a company like this is the stats you can get back, including how many people opened it, how many deleted it, and other information that can help you to shape your future marketing materials better, as well as determine if the ROI is worth this type of marketing strategy.

You can also sometimes use the list several times, doing different trials where you change the title or shift the marketing focus slightly to see what gets the best response. Getting feedback about your marketing through stats is another way these agencies can benefit your business.

Note that lists can be bought for one-time use or used multiple times throughout the year, as you offer different specials or products based on demand. The more seasonal your business is, the more you want to be careful about utilizing marketing options, including what agencies offer.

Additionally, you might be surprised at how many of these agencies are there when you go to exhibitions. As you build your network, you can also find companies to outsource different aspects of your business, thus enabling you to manage your costs effectively and, therefore, increase your ability to break even and eventually be profitable.

However, as your business grows, you might find it time to expand your team and hire staff. Let's discuss the best ways to do so without wasting time or capital.

Chapter 7

Building Your Team for Growth

Deciding to start a business can be daunting, but initially, your focus is on creating something viable. To keep costs down, you have likely been the one handling most of the daily operations. Perhaps you outsourced some tasks, such as your bookkeeping, warehousing, and fulfilment. Still, as the orders keep coming in, thanks to your marketing efforts, you realize the whole operation is getting too large for you to manage on your own.

The idea of growing your team might initially seem daunting. Who are you going to hire? How can you be sure they have the skills? What does that mean for your financials? Can the business support paying two or more people? What will it mean for overall profitability?

Having been in your shoes, I understand the process of building a staff. While hiring one person who knows how to do specific tasks might seem easier, it's crucial to have a contingency plan in place. What if they are sick or decide to move on to a different opportunity? This is why planning for such scenarios is as important as the hiring process itself.

Let's start by figuring out the best way to hire staff, especially if your company is not large enough to have its own human resources department.

For bonuses go to ...

Recruiting, Hiring, and Onboarding – The Start of Your Team

In the early stages of the business, you might find the staff you need by looking at family. Working with your family can have challenges, but my experience working in a family business is positive. My father and uncles worked together, and then I joined the business, working with my uncles. When dealing with a family business, each family member is focused on the business because it is more than a job. It is potentially the legacy of the family. The success or failure of the business plays a role in the financial success of multiple branches of the family, so there is definitely more at stake.

Depending on the type of business you are running, you might find necessary skills within your family that can be tapped to assist with the business. However, the boundaries of family and work can get blurred a bit, so having boundaries regarding roles is essential.

If you decide to take on a friend, this need for clear roles is still necessary. You have to be careful because you are changing the relationship dynamics by adding this professional layer. I work with a close friend, but we have been able to draw the line between personal and business. Although you have a certain level of trust with a family member or friend, there still have to be boundaries to separate the personal from the business, thus helping you to maintain the relationship.

However, you might not be able to find the skills you need with your family or friends. On the other hand, you might not feel comfortable hiring from within your circle. Regardless of why you hire outside of your circle, you might feel a bit overwhelmed when you begin the recruiting process.

One way to manage the recruitment of new employees is through an agency. These agencies typically run background checks and know the skills of the individuals they send to interview. They do a lot of vetting and narrowing down the CVs of individuals who meet your criteria, which can save you a lot of time and energy.

This process can be expensive, as you usually have to pay the agency a portion of their annual wage as a fee for their work. Essentially, you pay a fee before knowing if the person is the right fit, since these fees must be paid once you hire the individual.

For instance, you might be looking to hire a salesperson to expand your business. The individual whose CV shows they have handled millions of dollars/pounds in sales has the skills you are looking for, but they also had time with their previous companies to build a clientele. That clientele might not come with them, so they would start from scratch with your company. So, you would pay the agency but not necessarily see a return for months.

Additionally, you might still have to generate leads for them to follow, since they might not have any that they are bringing with them. Salespeople do have networks, but you have to know what you can expect initially before you decide to hire, especially when agency fees are involved.

Administrative hires can also be done through an agency, but you might opt to put an ad in your local paper if you are looking for someone local. Linkedin or other social media, which can cost

For bonuses go to ...

virtually nothing, is another possible avenue. Local job centers are also great places to find potential hires and are significantly more cost-effective. Advertising in trade magazines can also be an inexpensive way to find a highly qualified individual to join your team. Word of mouth is free and can lead to some great results. We were looking for an individual to hire for our warehouse, and one of our employees talked about it with her friend. That ended with us hiring her friend. Again, word of mouth costs nothing, and it can come with a bit of a recommendation, as in our case. The challenge is that if it doesn't work out, you might have a potential conflict with the person who introduced them.

If you opt to place an ad or otherwise complete the recruiting on your own, you must review the resumes, conduct background checks, call references, and complete the rest of the vetting process. While this is not impossible, it can take time and money. So, determining how you plan on recruiting and hiring is essential, as it can impact the financials of your business if not done correctly.

Temporary agencies might have a cost to them, but they allow you to try out an individual and see if they are a good match for your company before you complete the hiring process and take them on permanently. Regardless of how you choose to recruit your staff, it is essential to have a solid onboarding process in place, which will allow you to get them up to speed on their job requirements and training.

If you opt to do all the vetting yourself prior to hiring, make sure that you check their references. Although you want to believe that people are honest about their history, they are competing for a job and do not want to be judged as unable to handle the position. This could lead to them lying about why they may have left a previous position or about their skill set.

Checking someone's references and background assists you in determining whether they are being honest with you and are really up to managing the job effectively. Doing so can keep your business running smoothly as you transition from a team of one to multiple hires. However, what happens if you do everything you can to ensure a hire is a good fit, only to find that is not the case?

When a Hire Is Not a Good Fit

You might decide to hire an individual and expand your team; in the beginning, everything is excellent. The work is high-quality, and they seem to mesh well with you and the rest of your team. But as time progresses, what may have seemed like a good fit is no longer working out.

There could be several changes that you might have noticed:

- The quality of their work has declined.

- They were keen and had a good attitude initially, but their attitude is now off-putting.

- They procrastinate on tasks that were once done quickly without a fuss.

- They are missing deadlines.

For bonuses go to ...

- They seem distracted, even during meetings or phone calls.

You often reach a point where the quality of work and overall attitude has diminished so much that you question whether you want to keep them on or if it is time to let them go. If you keep them on, you may include additional training or a probationary period to see if their work and attitude can improve. But you need to set clear boundaries; otherwise, you may find yourself simply giving chance after chance with no concrete changes.

Taking on staff can be challenging, especially when the situation is no longer working out. You have to make the hard choices so that your business and the rest of your team do not suffer. A struggling employee can make it harder for the rest of the team, increasing the stress level and negatively impacting everyone else's workload.

Finding an employee can be costly. Keeping them on when they are not working out can also be expensive. When you choose to let them go, you incur the costs of finding another recruit and starting the process all over again. That also means you must handle the additional workload as you look for a new employee or pay your remaining employee additional money to do these tasks while you find a new hire.

I say this not to scare you from expanding your team, but to help you recognize that not every employee will be the perfect fit forever. You may find that your turnover reflects changes in family situations, health challenges, and a growing skill set that makes them no longer a fit for the job you hired them to do.

As your business changes, so will the job descriptions. Some members of your team may not be able to adjust to those changes, which can also create a need to change the team's dynamics.

If you decide to let someone go, you need to be sure that you follow all the legal requirements to protect your business, both legally and financially. Doing so can help you to shift direction with your team and have the right people in place as you grow, without damaging your company's reputation.

Deciding What to Pay for a Position

I have discussed cost several times in this chapter, mostly because I have come to realize that there are hidden costs in recruiting and hiring that no one talks about but needs to be aware of. Most business owners focus on figuring out the salary without considering all the additional costs related to recruiting and training.

But now that you have decided to make an offer to someone, you need to be clear about what you plan to have them do and what you plan to pay them.

There are several factors to consider when determining pay. The first is what your business can afford to pay someone based upon their skills and the job requirements. You know your financials better than anyone else, so you should be able to determine if the business is earning enough to pay for an employee. If the employee is a salesperson, you can look at their early salary as a cost of doing business. As they build a clientele, you should be able to justify their salary by the amount of business they bring to the table.

For bonuses go to ...

On the other hand, an administrative position does not provide sales income. Administrative staff perform tasks that keep your business functioning. Hiring administrative staff means having enough income to cover their salary and remaining profitable.

Once you know what you can afford, check out the average market rate for that type of job within your industry. That can help you determine whether your budget is below or above the market rate. If you are below market rate, you might want to explore what you can offer to make someone want to come and work for you.

For instance, a potential employee might turn down the lower market rate. Still, if you offer them an opportunity to learn new skills and have growth opportunities with your team, they might be willing to take the lower rate for the additional benefits you offer their career.

You also want to be fair with the salaries you offer to new members of your team. Staff talk to each other, so starting new members off at a wage significantly higher than what others are receiving could lead to resentment or conflict, especially if two people were hired for the same job with similar duties. The goal is to ensure that their salary reflects their experience and job requirements and is realistic for what your business can afford.

As time goes on, raises are also necessary. Today, many individuals find that annual raises are not enough to offset the cost of living. They can take their skills, move to another company, and see a significant salary raise. While you might be unable to match those offers, ensure your raises keep you competitive with the going market rate.

Additionally, a current employee who has been with you for years should not be making less than a new hire doing the same job. These tips will keep your business competitive in the overall job market as you look to adapt or expand your team. Raises also reward employees for doing a good job and incentivize them to keep up their efforts.

Managing Your Sales Team Effectively

Sales are the lifeblood of every business. Without them, you do not have any income, and the business eventually fails. However, managing a sales team comes with its own challenges. They are a competitive bunch. Bonuses and raises are often tied to their ability to meet specific sales goals.

When leads are generated and shared with the team, you want to be sure that they are shared equally and that customers are assigned to specific salespeople. We have software that generates leads and then assigns them to a particular salesperson. I find that customers will call up and have no idea who they might have spoken with. The result is that another salesperson could jump in and take the sale after another individual did all the work of cultivating the lead.

You need a system that effectively manages and assigns leads to avoid conflict and to create a culture where your team works together to meet sales goals. Understand that everyone on a sales team wants credit for the order, so having processes in place is vital to ensuring that your staff gets the proper credit for their work.

For bonuses go to ...

As part of managing your sales team, understand that businesses have periods where they are doing well, leading you to believe that you can take on more staff than you should. Then the business slows, and you are faced with figuring out how to pay everyone when you do not have the sales to support that team size.

You have to ensure that you have enough capital and work behind you to justify your staff if there is a sudden downturn in the industry. During COVID-19, for instance, many businesses found their sales dramatically decreased, leaving them with little choice but to lay off employees and close down part of their businesses. Other businesses opted to reinvent themselves in the face of restrictions, but that also takes capital.

I am not saying there will be another pandemic like COVID-19, but you need to expand your team with caution as a business owner. Study your financials and ensure that the sales are steady and that you have a capital reserve before starting a significant team expansion.

Preparing for the Unexpected

Downturns can happen to the best businesses, so capital reserves are key to helping you survive the low periods. Seasonal businesses, for instance, have to make enough money during the high periods to offset the costs of the slow seasons. Some businesses even reduce staff or other expenses and cut their hours of operation during those slower periods.

But what if only one person is trained to do a critical part of your process, and they become ill? Now, your business is scrambling to fulfill orders and keep customers happy while you are without a lynchpin from your team. How can you combat this potential issue?

Planning and cross-training are vital. Two people should be trained to complete every task or process in your company. This creates a contingency plan for the unexpected, thus keeping your business afloat until that employee returns to work, or you can hire a replacement.

Scheduling is also important. Everyone takes holidays, but you do not want everyone off at the exact same time. Working with your team, you can schedule holidays without leaving your team short-staffed. Consider using temporary agencies to help you manage tasks if you have a surge in business, or to cover when individuals are on leave or holiday. This can help you manage the work without increasing your staff.

Preparing to Expand Your Business

Beyond hiring staff, you might consider expanding your business to increase your market share and growth within your industry. That could involve purchasing additional space, hiring team members for the new location, or adding to your list of products and services.

I caution you to be careful and count the cost. Startups might have an influx of cash early on and decide to expand, only for the business to not meet the expectations set for it. In being prepared for

For bonuses go to ...

downturns in your business, you need to recognize that expansion might not be the only option available.

Ask yourself honestly if you need to expand your business at all. Some people have a great little business, but with the expansion, they take on a greater number of headaches, making it not worth the work in the long run.

For instance, we were in a set of service offices, where many costs of the space were included in the lease. Once we decided to expand to include a warehouse, our business was now responsible for the electricity, cleaning, and a host of other expenses. When you take on all those other expenses, you might find that your expansion brings in less profit than you anticipated.

You have to think very carefully about whether you really need to expand your business and if you have the money behind you to cover the greater level of expenses. If you do not need to expand, then you can maintain your profitability without adding to your expenses. Cost out any expenses and staff costs carefully before the expansion. If you are expanding into another location, you need to find trustworthy staff, since you will not necessarily see them from day to day.

However, other options exist to expand your business beyond adding a new location. Franchising allows you to receive a fee for using your products or services and takes the day-to-day activities off your plate. Think of local fast-food restaurants. Many are franchises, and although they pay regular fees to the main organizations, the company does not own that location. That means these organizations do not incur all the costs associated with running those locations but make an income from them.

Franchising has become extremely popular, with magazines and exhibitions devoted to helping people franchise their businesses. It is a way to increase the profitability of your business by giving you a share in another business. The best part is that you can franchise multiple locations without having to do anything more than train them in how to run their location.

Another option is taking on a partner. That can be full of risk, especially if the partner does not want to contribute at the same level that you are. In fact, if you do have a partner not contributing, it can be very difficult to undo the partnership without taking a financial hit, because now they own a financial piece of your business. Taking on an outside investor or going through a company that can help you by investing in your business is better. They take a share of the profits, but not ownership of your business. That investment can help you to expand without taking on all the risk.

Some businesses expand by buying out a competitor, gaining their customer base, product line, and even their equipment or property. The competitor might not be doing so well because they grew too quickly or for other reasons, but you can take advantage of that and use them to grow the reach of your own business.

You could also expand your product line or offerings. For example, if you sell one type of insurance, you could begin offering another type and sell that to your customers. They are more likely to purchase from you versus an online option, because they know and trust you due to their previous relationship with you.

Look for products that align with your existing activities. These could be products that are easy to sell to your existing customer base. By doing so, you can increase your business's overall profitability without necessarily adding a significant amount to expenses.

However, when it comes to expanding, adding staff members, or investing further into your business, you need a solid handle on your finances. In the next chapter, let's discuss your financials and what you need to be aware of as you strategize the next steps for your business.

Chapter 8

Understanding Your Finances to Get Profitable

Here is the harsh reality of owning a business: You can make a lot of sales, but if you do not understand how money is moving in and out of your business, you could be running at a loss. Our goal is for your business to be profitable, but that cannot happen if you expand too quickly or overinvest in capital, leaving your business no cushion.

Moreover, your financial acumen can be a powerful tool for strategic planning, guiding you on when to expand your team, invest in new equipment, or diversify your offerings. Understanding your financials can give you a clear picture of your cost per unit and fixed expenses. If these concepts seem daunting, fear not; this chapter is designed to demystify them for you.

Running a business doesn't mean you need to be an accountant, but it does require you to understand what information your financials provide and how to interpret it to determine whether your business is profitable. This chapter is here to help you achieve that understanding.

The Importance of Cash Flow and Reserves

Starting a business means having a certain amount of cash in reserve. You need to be able to cover downturns and early startup costs when sales income is limited. For instance, if you had a good month, you wouldn't think, "Let's go spend all the money." Instead, you would hold back some of that money in case sales slow down during the next month.

But how do you know if it has been a good or bad month? This is where your financial statements come into play. Financial statements are formal records that convey a company's financial activities and position. These statements provide essential information for decision making, whether for internal management or external parties, like investors or creditors.

The key financial statements are the following:

Balance Sheet – Provides an overview of your company's assets, liabilities, and shareholders' equity at a specific time. Assets include cash, accounts receivable, and other holdings. Liabilities encompass debts and obligations. Shareholders' equity represents the residual interest in the company.

Income Statement – Focuses on a company's revenues and expenses during a specific period. It also calculates net income by subtracting expenses from revenues.

Cash Flow Statement – Tracks how a company uses cash to pay debts, fund operations, and invest. It also reveals cash inflows and outflows.

You can evaluate your company's financial health and earnings potential using these financial statements. Regularly reviewing these statements is essential because, if you are going wrong, then you can quickly make changes to adapt. When you are familiar with your financial statements, you can pick up patterns that tell you where the areas of trouble are, which will assist you in adjusting specific areas, be it purchasing, sales, inventory, or administration.

If you ignore the financials, you can get way off course. Correcting that can be much harder, cost a lot more money, and potentially lead to you losing your business. Six months or a year down the line could be too late. Every month, you should review your financials, understanding how much was being spent, how much income was being generated, and how much you have in reserve.

How can you generate this information so that you have accurate financials? Today, many different software options allow you to input your expenses and income, as well as track invoices and categorize expenses. You can also outsource your bookkeeping but opt to use accounting software, which you and your bookkeeper can access.

Initially, you might opt to handle your bookkeeping using accounting software, but as business picks up, it could be time for a part-time bookkeeper. This individual can input all your financial information, including expenses. When working on your taxes, these accurate and up-to-date records can help you get back any money or deductions your business might be owed. You might not spend much on a part-time bookkeeper, but they are invaluable for determining where your business is financially.

Part of managing your cash flow involves more than just knowing where your cash is being spent; it also involves being disciplined about paying yourself. Initially, the business might only generate enough income to cover its expenses, without leaving anything to pay you. Therefore, you need to have a reserve of six months of your personal expenses so that you have cash to live on instead of spending the money that is coming into the business, thus running your business at a loss.

We have a show in the UK called Dragons' Den, similar to Shark Tank in America. Business owners looking for an investment come and pitch their businesses. Surprisingly enough, when these business owners come in and say they have been taking a salary, the experts are dead set against that. You simply can't be taking money out of the business for yourself before the business is making money.

The most important thing to remember is that you need enough money behind you to survive the business's early days and reinvest in the business to build a solid foundation for the future. My current business has doubled in size because I focused on returning all the available cash into the business. You might be surprised at the long-term benefits of reinvesting in your business.

If you are taking a journey, you need to plan how you will get there, when you will get there, and how much money you will be spending. There is planning involved. The same is true with your business. Defining your financial goals for your business and outlining expenses, overhead, and sales expectations will help you get there. Having a plan is key, but you should also share that plan with your accountant or friends. Their perspective can assist you in figuring out what the holes are in your plan, so that you can address them right away.

You have to have an idea of what the business is, how much it will cost, how you will make it profitable, and how you will support yourself in the meantime. The longer you can self-finance or have someone else finance you, the better the financial health of your business in the long run.

Be careful and make conservative financial decisions, to make sure that your growth is consistent. Operating lean versus taking on a significant amount of debt is often the key to long-term success.

To understand whether your business is running lean or not, you need to be able to understand or read your financial statement correctly. These are a window into your business. Your balance sheet is not likely to reveal any trends, but it will give you an overview of your assets, liabilities, and owners' equity on a specific reporting date.

The balance sheet is reviewed internally to give insight into whether the business is failing or not. An internal audience can shift policies, correct failures, give more resources to successful parts of the business, and pivot to better or new opportunities.

When the balance sheet is viewed externally by investors or other stakeholders, it gives insight into what resources are available and how those resources are financed. Potential investors can decide whether it would be wise to invest in your business or not. Lenders also look at the balance sheet to see if your business is healthy enough to take on additional debt.

Remembering that this information is tied to a specific date is important. A balance sheet is based upon past data by its very nature, but it can be used to predict future performance.

Your income statement, on the other hand, summarizes all your income and expenses in a defined period, including the cumulative impact of revenue, gain, cost, and loss. The purpose is to show your financial performance over a given period, and you can use this information to determine if the business is generating a profit. If your business spends more than it earns, it might not be profitable. Your income statements over time can show you when costs are highest, how much you pay to manufacture your products, and whether there is any cash to invest in the business.

There are two ways to analyse your income statement:

Vertical analysis – This means looking at one column of numbers, like a list of expenses, and seeing how each item compares to the total. It helps you understand the percentage of each item and makes it easy to compare financial reports from different times.

Horizontal analysis – This means comparing numbers from different time periods to see how they change. It helps you spot patterns, understand how well the business is growing, and see how it stacks up against competitors.

Utilizing both techniques can give you more insights into your business than simply doing one alone. Learning to read and understand an income statement can enable you to make more informed decisions about your business, especially if you are considering an expansion.

Finally, you have your cash flow statement, which provides a detailed picture of what happened to your cash during a specific period. This can show you if your business has the ability to operate in both the short and long-term. Think of it as a way to see whether you have enough reserves to weather a significant downturn or not.

Ideally, a company's cash from its operating income should routinely exceed its net income, because a positive cash flow speaks to the ability of your company to remain solvent and to have the ability to expand. Your cash flow statements also reveal whether a company is in transition or a state of decline.

Positive cash flow – Indicates a company has more money flowing in than out. Excess cash allows the company to reinvest, settle debts, and grow the business. However, that does not necessarily translate to profit.

Negative cash flow – Indicates your cash outflow is higher than your inflow, but it doesn't necessarily mean that profit is lost. Negative cash flow can be a result of expenditure and income mismatch during a specific period, and it should be addressed. You also might see negative cash flow when you decide to expand your business, so analyze cash flow changes from one period to another to get a better indication of how your business is performing overall.

Once you understand how to analyze your cash flow statements, you can clearly work though them to see the big picture of your company's finances. If you have questions, be sure to speak with your accountant. They can help you to understand what could be impacting the figures, as well as help you to identify trends to capitalize on.

Finally, you can use what you glean to create a financial business strategy as you analyze your financial statements. Keep in mind, as you review your financial statements monthly, you may need to tweak your strategy to reflect the changes in your business.

How can you create an effective financial business strategy? Start by assessing your current situation and evaluating existing financial processes and systems. Then define your goals with clear financial objectives that align with your vision. Consider growth, profitability, risk management, and innovation.

Then it would be best if you prioritize where resources will be allocated and balance the costs and trade-offs to support overall success. Embrace technology and efficiency, including leveraging AI, machine learning, and automation. Adapt to changing technologies and their impact on finance functions. Engage your team in digital efforts across finance, while fostering a culture of continuous learning and adaptability.

Remember, a well-crafted financial strategy drives growth, resilience, and innovation. With this understanding of your finances, you can create a strategy focusing on building your business and potentially expanding it. Let's explore what expansion can mean for your business, along with ways for you to take your business to the next level as you move to profitability.

This all may seem daunting to some people starting a business; however, there are many accountants and software that can make an easy job of this, at a small cost.

The important points are that the smaller the amount you take out of the business initially, the better health your business will be in. Once you have paid all your monthly costs, it's easy to see if your bank balance is growing, which is also a good guide to the financial health of your business.

We cover this in great depth in our mentoring program to show you how easy it can be to see where you are month by month—the satnav of your business to check that you are still on the right track.

Chapter 9

Do You Really Need to Expand?

The bigger your business gets, the more you have to manage. When it comes to your finances, expansion means more salaries, expenses, and potential debt. This is not to say that expansion does not have a place, but you need to be cautious about making the decision to expand.

Over the years, I have noted with many startups that early success leads to rapid expansion. Yet, just a few years later, the business is folding. Why? Because the income was not being generated fast enough to cover the rapid expansion. Then, when the expansion did not generate income, but the overhead and expenses kept rising, the business had to take on more debt to stay afloat.

This type of operation is not sustainable. When you create mounds of debt for your business early on, it can struggle to become profitable because so much of your income goes to expenses and debt payments. The trouble is that early success can make it difficult to remain patient, and slow to expand. But having self-discipline in the early stages of your business is often the key to your long-term success.

The beauty of building a business is that you make the decisions about expansion based upon metrics and specific milestones. For instance, you want to purchase equipment to increase your productivity and build your inventory. Instead of seeing that you have capital and making the purchase, you instead need to focus on whether or not the business has reached a specific sales threshold, thus allowing you to expand because the amount of sales justifies it, not because you have money to spend.

I have talked about expansion before in Chapter 7, but the focus was primarily on the costs and finding the right staff to assist you as the business grows. Now I want to talk about expansions specifically from the cost perspective, to help you understand the potential financial implications of expansion.

Why Do You Want to Expand?

For many businesses, expansion is seen as a sign of success, that your business is thriving, and that the demand is so high that you need more space, a larger number of staff, and a larger inventory. In the early stages of your business, you are focused on keeping the doors open, but once the demand for your products or services becomes apparent, you might shift gears and try to see where you can increase sales or have a faster fulfillment rate for current orders.

Let's talk about this in terms of a simple set of earbuds. You might sell an impressive set of earbuds, but people who order them have to wait three weeks to receive them. Expansion might mean increasing production so that your earbuds are in the customer's hands in less than a week. Part of your expansion at this point might also involve looking at how you ship orders and if there is a faster and cheaper way to get them from your warehouse to your customers.

Notice that there were two reasons to expand that would positively impact your business: it would bring about a better customer experience and potentially increase sales because you have the inventory to fulfill orders faster.

But can you support purchasing the additional equipment to grow your inventory? Can historical sales data demonstrate a high enough demand to justify the costs? Purchasing the equipment is just one part of the equation. You need staff to run that equipment and check to ensure the product's quality meets your standards.

We mentioned this before, but could you sell allied products to your existing customers? This could be a cheap win; happy customers might be pleased to give their reliable supplier additional business, and they will often even tell you what they are paying if you can help them save money—a win-win situation.

Sales do you no good if the products are consistently being returned due to defects. Do not expand so quickly that you sacrifice the quality of the products or services offered. I find that expansion can bring multiple issues in your business to the surface. First, if you are doing brisk sales but relatively small quantities, you might not need to be as consistent in following a process. But as you expand, processes become a lifeline for your business to create consistency for your staff and customers.

Do You Have the Processes Documented?

Expansion also means training new staff to handle the increased workload. When processes are in place and documented, it is easier to train your employees while also giving them a resource to follow the process step by step.

I find that processes are also crucial for consistency. Employees who have their own way of doing things can drive customers crazy because the customers never know what to expect from one experience to the next. Do you want to drive customers to your competitors? Lacking consistency is one way to do just that.

Processes are also essential if you are looking to franchise your business. Part of what makes your business unique is the customer experience. When you franchise, you want the brand's reputation to remain positive. Franchising with processes allows you to train your franchisees to give customers the same experience, no matter what location they are visiting.

Let's talk about American fast food again, because they have really mastered the franchise model. When you go to a McDonald's or Burger King, no matter what location, you have the same menu, and the food is cooked and prepared the exact same way. That level of consistency is what brings people back over and over again.

But they can't achieve that level of consistency without the right processes and training. Franchise fees are a great source of income, but you need to offer your franchisees something worthwhile. If they feel a lack of support due to inconsistent training and lack of processes, you will not be able to expand effectively.

Creating processes involves several steps. First, you need to identify your business goals, both current and long-term. Understanding what you want to achieve is vital to establishing procedures and processes that will help you to meet your milestones.

Next, you need a structured plan that outlines the procedures and processes necessary to achieve those goals. Break down high-level tasks into smaller, granular tasks. Use images, videos, and external resources to explain each detail.

When creating processes, you fill in the steps as you do them, but then have someone who does not do that task follow the steps. That will help you identify anything you might have forgotten to include, simply because it is so automatic.

Assigning tasks allows you to clearly define responsibilities for each step and ensure that everyone knows their role in the process. Then test the process by running a trial to identify any issues or bottlenecks. Make adjustments as needed. Once you complete the trials, start integrating the process into your daily operations. Train your employees on the new process and give them some time to adapt to the change.

Set key performance indicators (KPIs) to measure the success of your processes and procedures. These will help you monitor progress and identify areas for improvement. The KPIs will also give you critical feedback, allowing you to continuously evaluate and adjust the process based on that feedback and your business's changing needs. Remember, well-designed processes enhance efficiency and contribute to your success.

For bonuses go to ...

Maintaining Your Company's Culture

As your business grows, preserving your company's culture becomes crucial. How can you do this effectively? First, build your company's culture around a central theme that is easy to implement and recognize. For example, Apple is known for its user-friendly products and services that enhance the user's experience. The culture is evident, from an Apple store to corporate headquarters. That consistency is also apparent to the customers, giving them a quality experience that results in repeat business.

Your business also needs that level of consistency in its culture. Define the values, ethics, functions, coordination, and shared goals of your business and your teams. The prevalent system should remain consistent even as you deal with turnover within your team. Implement your system in the early days of your business, especially when the company is small.

Another way to maintain your corporate culture is to conduct social interviews and hire in groups. When adding new team members, consider group hiring. These social interviews help you to assess the cultural fit and alignment of potential employees with existing ones. Remember, maintaining culture during expansion ensures a cohesive and thriving organization.

Expanding your business is an exciting step, but it requires careful planning. Here are some key considerations to keep in mind:

Due diligence – Take your time to explore options and understand the opportunities available. Talk to experts, weigh pros and cons, and learn from others' experiences. Ensure your financial reserves are sufficient for what you are planning.

Know your numbers – Understand your financials thoroughly. Consider carefully the return you are making on investments, cash flow for big projects, and payroll sustainability. Anticipate disruptions and plan accordingly.

Quality matters – Don't compromise on quality during an expansion. Keep offering the same high standards that customers expect.

As you grow, maintain your company's culture because it impacts employee engagement, recruitment, and overall performance. Culture is as vital as your business strategy. When you understand the important aspects of your business and maintain them throughout your expansion, then your business can grow successfully.

How to Know It Is Time to Expand

One of the biggest challenges for any business owner is knowing when it is the right time to expand. After all, there are the financial considerations and the realities of growing too fast, only to have your business struggle or even close. But expansion can be a logical next step when you have several factors in place. Let's discuss what those are and how they can impact your business strategy for expansion.

First, do you have a loyal customer base? A strong, loyal customer base is a positive sign for expansion. Businesses create different locations or add to their offerings, hoping that their customers will support those changes and keep doing business with them. A loyal customer base is also a great source of feedback, letting you know if the changes are resonating or off-brand. Listen to your customers and craft your expansion to meet their demands.

Secondly, are you struggling to meet customer demand? Are your customers asking for more offerings from your business? These could be signs that you are ready to expand, thus capturing a more significant market share.

How can you effectively determine if there is enough customer demand to warrant expansion? Measuring customer demand is crucial for effective business planning. One key indicator is sales data analysis, which allows you to monitor sales trends over time. Analyze which products or services are consistently popular and which might need to be removed from your offerings because of a lack of interest. The goal is to keep turning your inventory, and as you expand, you want to keep offerings that meet customer demand. Also, look for seasonal patterns or spikes in demand, as that can assist you in determining if those spikes warrant expansion.

Other ways to measure customer demand include market research to understand your customers' preferences, needs, and buying behavior; web analytics that track website traffic, page views, and conversion rates; social media engagement, as high engagement rates can indicate demand; and inventory turnover rates, as high turnover suggests high demand. To determine if you have high turnover rates, calculate how quickly inventory sells out and needs to be replenished. Combining these methods provides a comprehensive view of customer demand for your offerings.

Once you have assessed the demand for your offerings, focus on the profitability of your business. Expanding will likely be viable if your business has consistently been profitable for three or more years. Again, this is a count-the-cost exercise. Just because you can expand does not always mean that you should. Financially, it has to make sense, but it also should be strategically done to meet your long-term goals for the business. Setting specific milestones can help you to determine if the business is really ready for this next step economically.

As I mentioned before, expansion involves hiring more staff, especially staff you can trust. Ensure you have the training in place to create a team capable of handling the expansion without a dip in customer service and the overall quality of your products. Finally, if your industry or market is expanding, then this might be the right time for expansion.

However, you might wonder what the next step is after you expand your business and reach key milestones. Let's explore what it means to step out of the role of hands-on business owner.

Chapter 10

Valuing, Selling, and Exiting a Successful Business

Exiting a successful business can be one of the most rewarding aspects of entrepreneurship. You have achieved a goal, built something from nothing, and now are ready to move onto your next adventure. But making the decision to exit can be difficult, especially when you have put so much time, effort, and heart into the process. This is where a mentor's guidance becomes invaluable. As a mentor, I understand that this is often the time when my students need the most help to ensure they get the best deal and avoid time wasters.

Whether you're looking to retire, pursue new ventures, or capitalize on your hard work, understanding how to value, sell, and exit your business is crucial. This chapter will guide you through the key steps and considerations to ensure a smooth and profitable transition.

Keep in mind, there are many ways to exit your business. You can opt to sell, hire management to run it while you step back, transition the business to one of your children, sell a portion but keep controlling interest, or do a management buyout. But to decide how you want to exit your business, you also need to figure out how you want to receive your payout. Some individuals looking to retire see having a controlling interest as a way to create a regular income stream. Others want to sell outright to start another business or become an angel investor for other startups. Regardless of why you choose to sell and what you plan to do once you exit your business,

I encourage you to speak with a financial advisor before you start the exiting process.

What to Consider When You Decide to Sell

So, you decide to sell your business and move forward to the next season of your life. But how do you know that it is the right time to sell? Or should you opt to step back from your business but retain some interest in it, thus creating a passive income stream?

Over time, you have built up your profits and likely have over 3 years of financials to demonstrate the success of this business. But you are ready to move on to retirement or build a new business. You want to cash out of your current business, but what is the best way to do so?

The first thing you need to do is figure out what your business is worth as that will determine which strategy you are likely to choose. This is done through a business valuation, a complex process that involves assessing various financial metrics and market conditions. The goal is to determine a fair price that reflects the business's true worth. By getting a valuation, you can determine if your business meets the criteria of your business plan and thus triggers your exit strategy.

Common Valuation Methods

How does someone determine the value of their business? Several different approaches could be used.

Asset-Based Approach: This method involves calculating the business's net asset value by subtracting liabilities from assets. It is often used for companies with significant tangible assets.

Income-Based Approach: This approach focuses on the business's ability to generate future profits. Key methods include:

Discounted Cash Flow (DCF): Projects future cash flows and discounts them back to their present value.

Capitalization of Earnings: Divides the expected annual earnings by a capitalization rate.

Market-Based Approach: This approach compares the business to similar businesses that have recently been sold. Common metrics include price-to-earnings (P/E) ratios and revenue multiples.

Financial professionals can complete each of these approaches. A local accountant can assess your business's financial health and provide valuation insights. They often focus on tax preparation and financial reporting. Valuation firms specialize in offering comprehensive valuation services. They analyze your financial statements, industry data, and comparable business to determine the value of your business.

Investment banking firms can provide valuation expertise, especially for larger transactions. They consider market trends, industry dynamics, and growth potential. Choosing the right professional depends on your specific needs and the purpose of your valuation.

For bonuses go to ...

Preparing for Valuation

Once you determine who will complete your business valuation, you need to prepare, making sure that you have everything they need to get the clearest idea of what your business is worth right now. Please keep in mind that valuations can change as industries shift and market demand changes.

Your business will need to ensure that its financial statements are accurate and up to date. Work with your bookkeeper and accountant to ensure that you have current income statements, balance sheets, and cash flow statements.

Operational data provides detailed customer base, contracts, and supply chain information. Obviously, you would want to keep your customer list confidential at this point, but you need to be able to show your sales and historical data that shows your business is viable.

Finally, your valuation professional should ask for information about your market position. You highlight your competitive advantages, market share, and growth potential here. What makes your business so special that it should be worth more on the open market?

After providing this information, the valuation professionals evaluate all the data to create a market value for your business. They will also review your expenses to determine what a new owner would have for expenses versus what expenses the business carries now.

For example, your business might currently pay for a company car for you and your family. However, the new owner will not have that expense, so it wouldn't be part of the business expenses for the valuation. The goal is to get a clear picture of what your business could offer a new owner in terms of profitability and growth potential, as both of those things impact its value in the eyes of a potential buyer.

Selling Your Business – Understanding the Process

When you put a house up for sale, there is plenty of advice on staging your home, the best time to put it on the market, and whether you should sell it using a real estate professional. Selling your business involves many of the same things. Let's dive into what you need to be mindful of during the process of putting your business up for sale.

First, you need to understand the importance of timing. Choosing the right time to sell your business is critical. Market conditions, economic cycles, and industry trends can all impact on the sale price. Ideally, it would be best if you sold when the business is performing well and market conditions are favorable.

Working with professional advisors can be key to determining if it is the right time to sell or if you should hold off because market conditions are not ideal. Engage a team of professionals, including a business broker, accountant, and lawyer, who will all guide you through this process.

I have found from experience that although a business broker generally does a good job, they want to introduce as many people as they can to you and your company.

It is vital that you know what your business is worth and what you are prepared to accept, which could be vastly different.

You need to ensure the broker knows realistically what you are prepared to accept and advise the potential purchaser. This will save a lot of time, not to mention you giving away sensitive information to a company just fishing to find out about your business, with no serious intention to buy your company.

Although it might seem important to keep your staff aware of the changes and potential sale, if they know too much, it could negatively affect how your business is running and reduce the chances of a quick and profitable sale. Maintain confidentiality to prevent disruptions in your business operations and to avoid alarming employees or customers. Once an offer is on the table and has been accepted, you will want to share information about the sale and the transition process to the new owner with your employees and customers.

Like the advertising and efforts made to draw attention to your house when it is for sale, you also need to develop a marketing plan to attract potential buyers. This includes creating a detailed prospectus that outlines the business's strengths and opportunities and financial information so that they can complete their own due diligence.

With the right marketing strategy, you will eventually have an offer or multiple offers. Now you have to negotiate the sale. That process starts with screening potential buyers to ensure they have the financial capability to complete the sale, and the right intentions for your business. This is essential if you are trying to create continuity for your employees and customers.

Additionally, knowing that the buyer has the financial capacity to complete the sale can play into what type of deal structure you agree to, and the financial implications for both of you regarding taxes and income.

Next, you have to negotiate the terms of the sale, including price, payment structure, and any contingencies. Common deal structures can include the following:

- Outright sale – The buyer pays the full purchase price at closing.

- Installment sale – The buyer pays over time, often with interest.

- Earn-out – Part of the purchase price is contingent on the business achieving certain performance targets post-sale.

Your deal structure needs to align with your future plans, thus creating the type of return you want to achieve. Remember that regardless of the deal structure, you and your team will have to participate in a transition, which allows you to train the new owners on the processes and procedures and introduce them to your team. With an earn-out deal structure, your team's performance can play a significant role in whether or not targets are met post-sale, so you must keep your team focused and allay any potential fears about the sale to maintain their productivity.

Of course, now that you have tentatively agreed to a buyer's offer, they can do their own due diligence. The buyer will conduct a thorough review of your business. Be prepared to provide extensive documentation and answer detailed questions about all aspects of your operations. They need to know that you have not falsified anything to make the business appear better than it really is.

For them, this business is a significant investment of their time and capital. However, during the due diligence, you also have a chance to showcase what makes your business viable and worthy of moving forward with the sale.

Exiting Your Business – The Transition Begins

Once both you and the buyer are happy with the terms of the sale, and the deal structure is in place, you need to focus on transition planning. Develop a transition plan to ensure a smooth handover. This may involve any of the following:

Training the new owner – Providing training and support to help the new owner understand the business.

Communicating with stakeholders – Inform employees, customers, and suppliers about the change in ownership and answer any questions regarding operational changes, if any.

Exiting your business also means planning on your part regarding the financial and tax considerations of the sale. Work with a tax advisor to understand the tax implications of the sale and explore strategies to minimize the tax liability. Develop a plan for investing the proceeds from the sale to secure your financial future.

In addition to the financial aspects of the transition, you also have to adjust to life after selling your business, which can be challenging. Consider how you will spend your time and pursue new interests or ventures. This involves working with a financial advisor to ensure you have a solid retirement plan in place.

However, many entrepreneurs relax for a period of time and then decide to dive back in and start a new business. Consider how your skills and experience can be leveraged into new opportunities. Regardless of how you choose to spend your time after you sell your business, make sure that you focus on self-care. It is a big transition to go from running a business to a life without that constant demand for your time and attention. Use this period to reset and get tuned into your next stage of life.

Valuing, selling, and exiting a successful business requires careful planning and execution. By understanding the key steps and considerations, you can maximize the value of your business and achieve a successful transition. Remember to seek professional advice and take the time to prepare thoroughly for each stage of the process. Exiting your business can be a rewarding experience that opens the door to new opportunities and adventures.

For bonuses go to www.theenterprisementor.com

Through my mentoring program, I can help you with anything from advising on retiring to starting another business or even buying a business. May this next stage of your journey lead to a profitable future for you and your business ventures.

About the Author

Stephen Frankel is an entrepreneur, author, business owner, and mentor with over 40 years of experience in starting and running profitable businesses. He founded Polypouch in 2011 and has consistently expanded that business. His clients include Unilever, 3M, Cadburys, United Biscuits, and Kraft Foods. Stephen shows companies how to get their products noticed with creative and versatile packaging.

Stephen recently acquired Surepak Ltd, expanding his family-run business to give his customers more options and increase market share. With his knowledge of packaging and sales, Stephen has built multiple profitable businesses, giving him a clear view of the potential pitfalls of business ownership and the opportunities available.

He has owned and run several businesses; some successful, some unsuccessful. After leaving school, working in a family printing business gave him the thirst to start and run his own business, inspiring Stephen to become an entrepreneur. He experienced many setbacks on his journey to success and wants to help people succeed by teaching them how to avoid the pitfalls, thus avoiding some stress as they build their businesses.

Stephen currently lives in the UK with his wife.

For bonuses go to www.theenterprisementor.com

Stephen can be contacted at enterprise@pobox.com or on his website www.theenterprisementor.com.

www.ingramcontent.com/pod-product-compliance
Lightning Source LLC
Chambersburg PA
CBHW052054070526
44584CB000178/2179